PRINCESS
IN LOVE

PRINCESS IN LOVE

ANNA PASTERNAK

A DUTTON BOOK

DUTTON

Published by the Penguin Group
Penguin Books USA Inc., 375 Hudson Street, New York, New York 10014, U.S.A.
Penguin Books Ltd, 27 Wrights Lane, London W8 5TZ, England
Penguin Books Australia Ltd, Ringwood, Victoria, Australia
Penguin Books Canada Ltd, 10 Alcorn Avenue, Toronto, Ontario, Canada M4V 3B2
Penguin Books (N.Z.) Ltd, 182-190 Wairau Road, Auckland 10, New Zealand

Penguin Books Ltd, Registered Offices:
Harmondsworth, Middlesex, England

Published in the United States by Dutton, an imprint of Dutton Signet,
a division of Penguin Books USA Inc.
Published by arrangement with Bloomsbury Publishing Limited.

First Dutton Printing, October, 1994
1 3 5 7 9 10 8 6 4 2

Picture Sources
I. Burns/Camera Press: page 5; Glenn Harvey Picture Collection: page 2;
Mirror Syndication International: page 4 top; Rex Features: page 8

ISBN: 0-525-94017-0

Printed in the United States of America

This book is printed on acid-free paper.
∞

To my grandfather, Frederick Pasternak

Acknowledgements

This book could not have been written without the unflinching support of my mother. My heartfelt thanks go to her for her wisdom and her sense of humour which I frequently relied upon.

I would like to thank my literary agent, Patrick Walsh, for his patience and stamina, and David Reynolds and Penny Phillips for their sensitive editing and kindness.

Finally, I am grateful to my father, who long ago instilled in me the self-discipline that was so necessary in the writing of this book.

Anna Pasternak
September 1994

Author's Note

I first met James Hewitt two years ago and gradually, over the ensuing months, as a mutual trust developed, I learned the true story related in this book. Once the disintegration of the Prince and Princess of Wales's marriage had become public knowledge, it seemed to me that the love that Princess Diana had shared with another man was too special to remain secret.

Not knowing the truth, the world has condemned James Hewitt. Now the truth can be known: that his love, support and encouragement played a vital role in helping the Princess of Wales through her marriage breakdown and enabling her to develop the inner strength she displays today.

Theirs was a love that arose through force of circumstance; I hope that this book, in showing why and how they were drawn together, will contribute to a proper understanding of and sympathy for Princess Diana and her position as mother of the future King.

1

A froth of self-satisfaction filled the room. Women cosseted by wealth and position, sleek in smart suits and statement jewellery, tossed their heads alluringly for confident men with expansive body language and studied nonchalance. The mood was exuberant, the air alive with the fizz of irrelevant party chatter.

When the Princess of Wales entered that Mayfair drawing room in the late summer of 1986, none of the assembled crowd – courtiers, titled grandees, fast, eligible young blades and their safe, pretty girlfriends – would have dreamed of breaking off conversation and publicly displaying even the slightest flicker of awe. Nevertheless, an almost imperceptible collective ruffling of feathers could be detected as everyone noted that they were at exactly the right place to be.

From the moment he caught her entrance Captain James Hewitt was aware of Diana. Not in the gawping, let's-assess-her-from-head-to-toe way, but with a protective sense of excitement and relief. Silently he watched her mingle, drinking in her effortlessness, her vibrant sheen and the way she cupped hands, tilted her head and generously, laughingly, gave everyone something to take away: a look, a smile, a bubble of conversation and, most impressive, the rare gift of sincerity.

With his acute sense of *noblesse oblige*, James returned his attention to the fey, wispy blonde with whom he was half-heartedly flirting, made a valiant attempt to spruce up the conversation, and offered to get her another glass of champagne. Just as he was proffering it, his host grabbed his arm. Leading him across the room, he told James that there was someone he wanted him to meet: 'Come on, I'll introduce you to Diana.'

As they approached her, James's heart might have been pounding with the thrill of anticipation but what struck him, from the second he shook her hand, was an overwhelming sense of familiarity. How utterly right it all seemed. Of course this was a beginning but he felt as if he were treading a well-worn path, comfortable in the knowledge that he knew the camber. Intuitively he knew both the deceptive crevices and the effortlessness of the plain, untroubled ground; he knew exactly where, and where not, to tread.

Fortunately, the noise and energy levels were soaring up to meet the ornate, vaulted ceilings, so no one noticed their rapt attention as they faced each other with a measure of shock and disbelief. There was no mistaking it; they both knew. Suddenly every nerve-ending was raw and dangerously alive.

In a hurried bid to gain composure they chatted frantically, marvelling at the ease with which conversation came. There were no awkward pauses, no searching for subjects. They were too hungry to learn about each other, too keen to devour those insignificant details that speak volumes when you need to know.

Diana was showing her most dazzling public face. Naturally she was aware of her magnetism but here, suddenly, was a man whom she actually wanted to captivate. Her desire, as she told him later, both frightened and excited her. Most men were attracted to her golden aura but blinded by it. They were dazzled but dared not touch. She was unaccustomed to meeting a man who allowed his interest to show, who, rather than trail behind in deference, was bullishly taking the conversational lead.

Unlike many in his military world, James Hewitt had no fear of, and genuinely liked, women. His flirtatious gambit was to chide gently, to couch his flattery in caressing teases and a warm, ready smile. Diana returned the compliment, rather straining to do so as she was out of practice. Not for a long time had she wanted to appear so vivacious and enticing. She felt so secure, wrapped in his kind attentive gaze, that almost before she was aware of it, she found herself opening up to him, talking honestly about herself, and greatly enjoying an all too rare opportunity. It was like cycling down a steep hill: at first it is smooth and easy, then, as the gradient tips, exhilarating, and finally, by the time you have brushed away that first wisp of fear, your momentum has gathered to such a pace that it would be more frightening to brake than just to let go.

Within half an hour, having ascertained that James was a Staff Captain in the Household Division with responsibilities that included running the Household Division stables, Diana had told him of her deep fear of riding. She explained that she had had an accident as a young girl while out riding with her sisters and her nanny. She had fallen in the grounds of Park House, the Spencers' Norfolk home, had hurt her arm and lost her nerve.

She said that although she had not enjoyed riding as a child, the fact that she had plenty of opportunity to do so now, having married into a thoroughly equestrian family, had made her decide that she would dearly love to conquer her fear. She wanted to do so for her own satisfaction, she stressed, not to suit anyone else – merely to regain her strength in the saddle.

James leapt for the bait. He would be delighted, in fact nothing would give him greater pleasure, he said, than to help the Princess rebuild her confidence. He was a skilled horseman, and his mother ran a riding stables in Devon. He assured her that he was eminently qualified for the job. It would be easy and within his military capacity, he explained, to arrange a series of lessons for her at Knightsbridge Barracks, so convenient for Kensington Palace.

United by a conspiratorial wave of relief at having so quickly and efficiently found an excuse to meet again, they parted and rejoined the bubbling throng of the party. Diana had promised that she would telephone him, and he knew that he would nurse his secret with the discretion that was the underlying condition of their friendship – a condition that was so glaringly obvious, it could be left unspoken.

That night, after the party, James did not just take any remotely beguiling young girl out to dinner as he would normally have done, but returned alone, harbouring an unfamiliar euphoric glow, to his South Kensington bachelor flat and went straight to bed.

Since his early twenties, when he started playing polo for the Life Guards, James had had regular contact with the royal family. Throughout his school career at Millfield his sporting prowess – he played polo, fenced, point-to-pointed and shot – bred an unshakable confidence in the outdoor world which he soon discovered was equally powerful indoors. As his acute sense of protocol rested on impeccable manners, it never occurred to him to feel anything but utterly at ease in the presence of Prince Charles, whom he admired and liked enormously.

Once, after a particularly rumbustious match at Smith's Lawn, when the players were united by their self-congratulatory sense of exhaustion and fun, James asked the Prince back to his rented flat in Ascot for tea. Prince Charles gently declined but asked his fellow sportsman to join him for a quick drink in the pavilion; a tiny but solid gesture towards friendship.

Remarkably for a man whose rigid, military upbringing had fed a simple, pragmatic approach to life, James's entrée into the royal milieu precipitated a strangely potent sense of destiny. He became aware of Lady Diana Spencer slightly sooner than the rest of the world through the polo fraternity, and inexplicably he always knew that he would meet her and get to know her. It was as if, slowly but surely, unseen hands were pushing him through life towards her, his experiences being mapped out to prepare him for her.

His first tangible sense of her was in 1981, when he was playing polo at Tidworth for the Army against Prince Charles who was representing the Navy. The young Diana Spencer had come to watch her fiancé, and the world had come to watch her. For the first time in public she buckled under the strain of the engagement – not, as she told James later, so much because of the zeal of the press as because of the nauseous fear continuously washing over her that her relationship with Charles was not as it should be. Try as she might, she could not shake off the ghosts that persecuted her incessantly, telling her to embrace the truth before it was too late. On one level she already knew that the depth of her own love was not matched, yet she did not have the strength to cope with the lacerating disappointment of facing it.

As her thin, weary frame crumpled against the car and the tears ran unguarded down her face, it was not her future husband's heart that ached in empathy but James Hewitt's, as he watched from his mount. Disturbed that her sadness was so heavy and so profound, he would gladly have taken her misery from her and, in any way possible, eased her load. But, of course, it was impossible. For once he let his competitiveness drift, and the goal he scored against the Prince meant nothing to him; it only made things worse.

From that moment on he was conscious that he was aware of Diana wherever she was in the world. Although he didn't give it much credence, he was in fact deeply moved by the apparently idyllic picture the Prince presented with his fairy-tale bride. When the royal couple were on their honeymoon, cruising round the Mediterranean, James was following their every move with, perhaps, an unnatural degree of interest. Stationed in Cyprus, he found his concentration swallowed up by the azure sea as he stared at the horizon and fought off an almost uncontrollable urge to wire the royal yacht *Britannia* with a message of his greetings.

It was not that he wanted to disturb Charles and Diana, more that he wanted a speck of the magic dust that seemed to surround them for himself. He may have been intuitively aware of Diana's vulnerability, but he firmly believed that she had found her prince; it was an image that touched and delighted him.

James had never allowed himself the luxury of wondering if he was a romantic – that would have seemed foolishly self-indulgent – yet he was sufficiently sensitive to know that his life had been all but devoid of romance.

That he had a twin sister, another sister eighteen months older than himself and an adoring mother meant that from an early age he was made acutely aware of women and their needs. He had no brothers and during his youth did not see a great deal of his father, a Royal Marine, because either he was away at sea or James himself was away at school. However, even from a distance James was ruled wth strict discipline. It was not that John Hewitt was an ogre, a gratuitous taskmaster, but James was never left in any doubt that if his father required something of him, he should do it.

His early childhood, spent in a large redbrick house in Kent surrounded by paddocks and horses, was good and old-fashioned. His parents hunted regularly with the East Kent and theirs was a ruddy, sporting existence. James felt eminently secure, as the rigid code of manners he was raised to adhere to left no room for doubt. He knew exactly how to treat people: you addressed a man as 'sir', and if a woman entered the room you stood up, pulling out her chair for her if she was to sit at the table.

Perhaps it was unfair to send him to the progressive public school Millfield, where in his country tweed jackets he was generations apart from his contemporaries who, in their vivid flares and stacked shoes, revelled freely in the sartorial ease of the seventies. It never occurred to James to try to be something that he was not. He remained steadfastly in his fawn cavalry-twill trousers, striped shirt and tie; that was what his parents expected, so that was how it had to be.

For the first time he felt different and shy. His excruciating politeness, far from winning admirers, acted as a barrier that further alienated him from the crowd. He had been prone since childhood to shutting off emotionally: in the Hewitt household anything approaching a feeling was exercised away or swept under the carpet. James preferred to ignore his feelings, and settled down instead to the serious business of sport and mildly laddish fun.

He was far too sensitive to women to be of any interest to teenage girls. Scared to attempt a kiss in case he upset the girl, he did not have a girlfriend until he was nineteen. It was not

16

something that bothered him unduly; in his calm, patient way he trusted that when the moment came, it would be right.

When it did, it was. Safe at home, and far from the pressures of prying eyes and schoolyard tales of conquests, one evening, having picked up the determined message in her eyes and noticed the more than accidental physical contact in the stables, James boldly invited one of his mother's riding pupils for a drink.

That his first affair was not a fumbled, hurried event, pregnant with embarrassment and confusion, meant that James immediately learned to respect and cherish women physically. His first partner was, at twenty-seven, eight years his senior and a mature, educated, pretty young woman. He soon became a skilled, adventurous lover.

He may have spent the next decade playing out his new-found expertise, hurriedly making up for his barren teens in a healthy, endearing manner with a galaxy of suitably flighty girls, but by the time he was twenty-eight and lying in bed wondering when the Princess of Wales would call, he knew that this was the first time that love had entered his adult life.

His emotions were rapidly knitting into an unfamiliar blanket. His head was shrieking at him to cast it off, while his heart was quietly telling him to lie down and allow himself to be cosseted by this strange new warmth. He was comforted by the knowledge that his initial suspicion, just a few months before, that he was truly in love, had been correct. Now, at least, the fear that his imagination was reaching absurd and unruly heights could be laid to rest.

For James Hewitt did not lose his heart when his rapport with Diana was so unerringly established at that fateful Mayfair drinks party, but on the day of the Duke and Duchess of York's wedding, in July of that same year.

There was nothing that gave this eager captain of the Life Guards greater satisfaction than the opportunity to flex his army muscle and put his military training into operation. Born and bred for duty, he was calmly fulfilled by his intention to spend his life honouring it. On the morning of the Yorks' wedding he had risen early to join Selina Scott on *Breakfast Time* on television to explain his role for the grand day. His flirtatious ebullience and risqué eye contact had soon brought a coy smile to Selina's lips. Despite the leaden hangover that was threatening to mar his morning, he had described his co-ordinating duties, coherently explaining that he had to help with the orchestration of the various bodies of troops that were involved throughout the day.

Buoyed up and amused by his fluent television appearance, the flush of adrenalin and self-importance rising in his cheeks, he was soon marching briskly round Buckingham Palace, where he was in charge of security. Suddenly alone, he found himself in an area where he probably should not have been – and there, sitting barefoot on the stairs, was the Princess of Wales.

In that unguarded moment he saw just how lovely she really was, how natural and relaxed as she sat there unaware that she was being watched, chatting with a small group of staff, laughing and animated. Hugging herself with her knees scrunched up under her chin, her fingers dancing across her naked toes, she took his breath away. No memories of his ceremonial duties would outlive the snapshot of happiness he caught that day.

The call came sooner than expected. James was studiously dealing with paperwork at his meticulously tidy desk in his Knightsbridge Barracks office overlooking the leafy expanse of Hyde Park. He had not yet reached the stage of feeling excited every time the telephone rang in the hope that it might be her, because he had not envisaged that she would contact him for quite some time. He knew how busy her schedule was, and he had wasted a lot of time endeavouring to convince himself that he would be a long way down her list of priorities.

He was wrong and he knew it. A few days after their meeting she telephoned. Was he serious, she asked, about the possibility of his giving her riding lessons? Of course, he laughed, every inch a man of his word, and again he stressed that he was only too happy to be of assistance.

'That's settled, then,' she replied, exhaling a sigh of relief. 'As soon as you can fit me in, I will be there.'

As he put down the receiver, he allowed a rare wave of excitement to course his body. He had not realised that it would be so wonderful to hear her voice again. The warmth that had emanated from her during their conversation was undeniable. Before he allowed his charged thoughts to obliterate the rationality that was his backbone, he stood up and strode out of his office to set the necessary course of arrangements into motion.

He went straight to his commanding officer, Lieutenant-Colonel Morrisey Paine, a dapper little man with a relaxed sense of fun, and explained that the Princess of Wales would like to come to the barracks in a low-key, unofficial capacity to learn to ride. He would instruct her early in the morning so that it would not interfere with his duties, starting in the indoor school and then, if all went well, progressing to the breadth of Hyde Park.

Paine must have known that Hewitt, with his indefatigable sense of decorum and duty, was just the right man for the job. Hewitt's studied seriousness and air of gravity were assurances that this was a task he would carry out as efficiently as any other, with the minimum of fuss. He could be relied upon to respect the delicacy of the affair and not to brag to the other officers. Providing everybody knew their place and stuck to it, it seemed a perfectly splendid idea.

Both Diana and James sensed that this was the start of an adventure, and it excited them. The minute she saw him standing waiting for her in the stable yard, tall and assertive, she felt at once tense and relaxed. She had forgotten the strength of her attraction to him and how, far from threatening her, he made her feel both wilfully feminine and yet reassuringly safe. She was aware of his desire for her and, rather than refuse to react to it as she normally would have, brushing it away as if it was a fly that had mistakenly landed on her forearm, she felt empowered. She was intrigued. She had not felt this much at sea, but confident that she was swimming the right waters, for what seemed an eternity.

Ever since she had watched Prince Charles play polo in the days of their courtship, and been consumed with admiration for his physical ease, she had found men in uniform attractive. James was certainly no exception, with that strain of lean muscle that comes only to men who work daily to look after themselves. She could not help but be struck by his appearance.

Sensibly, he gave Diana and her lady-in-waiting a perfectly balanced welcome, displaying equal courtesy to both. Diana had arranged for Hazel West to accompany her for her riding lessons as she was the only one of her ladies-in-waiting who could ride. Tall, blonde and whippet thin, Hazel was blessed with the innate elegance that can never be bought or acquired. Married to Colonel George West, a retired Grenadier Guard who worked in the comptroller's office at St James's Palace, she was eminently suited to court life and, naturally vivacious, enjoyed an easy friendship with the Princess.

As James went to find Diana a suitable horse – a quiet grey whose plodding good nature would not unnerve or undermine her – he had no idea that he was triggering what was to become a long process of nurturing. And as he helped her to mount, attending to the length of her stirrups and making sure that the girth was tight enough to make her feel secure in the saddle, she was, as she later confessed to him, flooded with emotion and relief that here, suddenly, was a man with time for her.

With a rush of sadness she realised that she had spent so long trying to placate her husband, so many years trying to win his attention and earn his love, that she had forgotten what it felt like to be given unconditional attention. She may have had the world at her feet, but what good was that when she craved affection from the one man who seemed unable to give it to her? With his measured concern and genuine desire to help, James could little have known that he was coming close to the chord in Diana that she had long ached for someone to touch.

An experienced instructor, James felt supremely confident in his capacity as teacher to Diana. Instinctively he knows how to get his charges to relax, by chatting and issuing gentle commands. He did not stand in the centre of the schooling ring barking staccato military orders, but casually yet firmly coaxed the best out of her.

When she came out of the saddle, an hour later, the balance of power still lay with James. His authoritative air of charm and optimism had worked wonders and he assured Diana that he would have her jumping bareback in no time. The ease with which they joked and the sparkle of their communication underlined the silent communion between them that was gathering its own momentum.

As the riding lessons progressed, so the phone calls proliferated. To his delight, James found that his days were regularly disturbed by Diana fixing their next lesson or arranging to slip another into her crowded schedule. By now they were meeting once or twice a week and, with a wry smile of benevolent amusement, he registered how many of her calls were professionally not strictly necessary. But just as she seemed to need to keep in touch, he too welcomed the chance to hear her voice.

Once Diana had mastered the rudiments of the saddle again and found her confidence returning as James's solidity dissolved her nerves, they started to ride out in the crisp early mornings round Hyde Park. Initially they were flanked by a fug of police and plain-clothes detectives, but gradually Diana insisted that they drop away.

Usually she rode ahead with James, followed by Hazel West and often Major-General Sir Christopher Airey who was commanding the Household Division and who, along with the detectives, kept a discreet distance. Diana adored the tall, debonair Major-General (whom Prince Charles was later to part company with as his private secretary, perhaps because of Airey's perceived sympathy for Diana). With his watery blue eyes and sleek grey hair, he was just the type of distinguished-looking, kind and amusing elder statesman that she felt comfortable with.

As she hacked around the park, sharing with James the pleasure of seeing the shafts of early sunlight striking the gently lapping water of the Serpentine, she felt happier than she had felt in a long time. These meetings, she was soon to tell him, were becoming an integral and much-needed release from the tension that characterised her daily life.

She realised that as she was building up her trust in James as a teacher, she was also developing her faith in him as a man. With him she could breathe again and for a short time allow the stress to fall away a little. His quiet, undemanding manner allowed her to unfurl at her own pace and, as they discussed the ambiguous minutiae of their daily lives, she found herself struggling not to tell him the whole sad truth.

Instead, she focused on him. Did he have a girlfriend, she asked – trying, he thought, to seem uninterested. When he told her that there was no one special, her shoulders dropped in relief and she teased him about the ready string of girls he presumably had waiting in the wings. Innocently, he laughingly recounted the pattern of his bachelor days, completely unaware that the thought of him with another woman inspired a fresh layer of the protective jealousy that was already ripping Diana's life apart.

She may have failed with her husband, but here was a man whom she might secure for herself and she determined to do so. Unable even to consider the possibility of getting close to a man if he had the potential to reject her, she would make sure that, in time, James was aware of every hour that she had thought she was drowning in her own loneliness before he touched her.

Yet constantly she was forced to reprimand herself, to keep her impulsive, giving nature in check. She must *not* tell him what was going on. If he knew the truth, she worried, he would be shocked. He would not find her as attractive, and she just could not bear that. It was essential that she keep up her bubbly, carefree façade. In order not to strangle the possibility of her growing closer to James, she presumed, she had to keep the myth of her life alive.

If she had only stopped to analyse him thoroughly she would have known sooner that he did not care about such things. To him, with his trenchant honesty and pure code of honour, the world was black and white. You stood by and protected your friends, regardless of the cost.

It was a theory that was soon to be tested to – and indeed beyond – all conceivable limits.

It had become customary after their morning rides for James and Diana to dismount and, once the horses were in safe hands, to saunter into the Officers' Mess for a cup of coffee. Both looked forward to this relaxed moment of near intimacy almost as much as to the invigoration of their rides. For Diana, the physical proximity to James and the opportunity to bask alone in his soothing aura had become one of the mainstays of her existence.

That particular morning, she had found it difficult to concentrate. It was taking all her supple will-power to ensure that her valiantly cheery face did not slip. Her whole body felt cumbersome, stiff and heavy from the dull ache of suffering that had become part of her.

She watched James and his eager affection for his horse and for the day – for life, in fact – with envy. He seemed so pure and uncomplicated. His was surely the easier existence, was it not? A lighter world where the constant self-analysis and worried monitoring of every change of mood and flicker of emotion was never even considered. His emotional life seemed, like a healthy heart monitor, to keep a steady pulse, whereas hers could suddenly and quite erratically shoot up or down, the jagged peaks and dangerous troughs frightening and exhausting her.

Ever since she was a girl and friends came to stay at Park House, she had felt different. They all seemed so robust, so self-sufficient, their attentions focused on the television and their suppers, studiously unpacking their overnight bags and casually flinging on their nighties before leaping into bed. They seemed quite unburdened, genuinely content to be away from home, secure in the knowledge that the status quo would be exactly the same on their return. They, the young Diana felt, trying to control her jealousy, did not know what it was like to live with that degree of uncertainty, that ghastly spectre of worry.

Diana might have appeared self-contained and in control to the stream of nannies who tried to instil discipline and thereby

stability in her life after her mother, Frances Roche, had left
her father, Viscount Althorp, for the debonair businessman
Peter Shand Kydd – but inside her heart was breaking. She
felt that the very foundations of her life had been destroyed.
All the values that she had expected to live her life by – a
happy marriage and a jolly, rambling family, with a husband
who would catch your eye across a room and know what you
were thinking until the day you died – had been shattered. The
shock, like an unexpected slap in the face, was to smart for
years to come.

How could she have known then, at the age of six, that the
deep-seated layers of anger and confusion would not surface
until later, when she had the trigger of her own disintegrating
marriage to release them and a measure of the will and maturity
to deal with them? As a girl, lacking the requisite emotional
coping skills, she buried the burning hurt and disappointment
and pretended – even tried to fool herself as often as possible
– that she was happy.

It was not in her nature to express anger. Somehow she felt
that to tear the roof down with her wails of frustration and
agony, or to scream until the pain dissipated, was wrong and
that she would be condemned as spoilt and greedy. She was
desperately upset, but what right had she to consider her own
feelings, she told herself, when her parents were hurting and
bleeding as well?

She thought that if she picked up the great parcels of their
guilt and carried them on her own weak back, she could
alleviate their suffering and somehow she would be vindicated.
She could not bear to see their agony, the pain etching fine lines
around her mother's sparkling blue eyes. She was so proud of
her mother's porcelain beauty, her soft elegance and her gentle
smiles; these qualities represented security and a blueprint for
the future. Seeing the grey film of anxiety stretched taut across
her face made Diana nervous, even more insecure.

And her father. She loved him so. His warm affability, his
soft, kind face. She loved his distinguished, portly bearing,
the old-fashioned timbre of his vowels. She understood his
weakness. His vulnerability reached out to her daily, extending

a needy hand, a hand she felt proud to hold in hers. It made her feel useful, important.

She was not sure whether her older sisters, Sarah and Jane, were in the same state of distress. They were mostly away at school or filling the house with friends and the camaraderie that made up those weekend house parties. That they seemed so grown-up, laughing and joking with hordes of admiring young men, whose wealth afforded them a certain carelessness, merely served to increase Diana's sense of isolation. She did not want to remind them of the frailty of youth, of the delicacy of her age, by pestering them with her unhappiness, so she locked it away.

Only at night, or occasionally when she was sitting alone staring into the abyss of contemplation at the bottom of the swimming pool, would she allow herself to express her grief, and there were times when she feared that the emotion she released would suffocate her.

She had to be strong for Charles, though, her brother who was young enough to know no shame and would lie in bed at night sobbing for his mother. Her maternal instincts on fire, Diana would go to him and, hugging him close, pray to take his pain. She could just about cope with her own, but watching the agony of tears scarring the sweet, innocent face of the brother she loved so much was more than she could bear.

James was aware that he had lost her. Physically she was right there beside him, carefully holding the reins, her posture correct and her gaze steady and firm ahead, but he knew that she was in a place to which he had no access. Sensitive enough to register the mood swings beneath her sunny mask, he could almost touch the sadness welling up inside her. His natural instinct was to go to comfort her, but he knew that it was too soon. That was not yet his role.

He pondered the cause of this sadness. Here she was, the most beautiful woman he had encountered, so adored by everyone, her charisma fêted by the world, with everything to sing for. Surely the horizon could only be clear? Why, then, did he see intermittent flashes of desperation discolouring her face?

Pushing such thoughts firmly aside because they were too arduous to contemplate was exactly how James usually dealt with emotional uncertainty. He was unaccustomed to running his finger along the knife-edge of his feelings. He was supremely diffident when it came to navigating from his head to his heart. It was so much easier to block off.

Returning to the busy task of cheering her up, he suggested that they retreat from the brisk morning air and the splendour of the park, which he suspected might somehow be precipitating this melancholy, and return to the barracks for coffee.

Usually they collapsed on the faded chintz sofa with ease, cupping their hands around mugs of steaming coffee to warm their stiff fingers, and spent a quiet minute surveying the military elegance of the room with its cabinets of gleaming trophies and endless silver decorations.

But today Diana had eyes for nothing. All she could see was the tunnel of misery stretching ahead of her. It was dark, she felt trapped and her fear was palpable.

Acutely aware of this and unable to stand it, James quietly enquired what was the matter. She must forgive him, he said, for asking, but he could not help noticing her obvious deep unhappiness and it troubled him. If there was any way that he could help her, if there was the slightest thing that he could do, he added, she must know that he would be only too willing to do it.

Unable, for a second longer, to hold herself back, Diana leaned towards him, her body almost buckling under the weight of the strain that she had carried alone for so long, and slowly she told him the truth.

What you have been reading in the papers is true, she said. All the endless speculation and media frenzy that my marriage is a sham is correct. It has been falling apart for years. My husband and I lead virtually separate lives.

Too fragile to cry, she felt that she dare not untap the well of tears within her, for once she unleashed them, they would never stop. She did not know, she told him, where the base of her unhappiness lay but she suspected that it was buried so deep that she would never have the strength to get to it and unearth it.

As she continued talking, her voice strangled by the misery of her words, James held her with his eyes and his heart.

He could not believe what he was hearing. He was utterly shocked, the very core of him reeling in disbelief. How could it be true? How could this wan, exquisite creature be so unhappy? He did not think he had ever been anywhere near such violent unhappiness in his life, and it frightened him.

His brow furrowed with concern, he sat rigid, concentrating hard. He heard what she said, that Prince Charles did not love her, that with the weight of the Prince's family behind him she was an outcast at the Palace, alienated and trapped. That she had tried everything in her power to make it work, throwing herself into her duties with a tenacity that she had not known she was capable of, and that still, all the time, instead of praise, only criticism was levelled at her, the harshness of which had finally cracked her spirit.

She was like a frail bird whose wings had been torn apart, who no longer had any hope of flying or enjoying any freedom again. To stay alive, she knew she had to talk. She could not go on living in the murky shadow of her secrets, secrets that were threatening to consume her. And here beside her was this man, this man who seemed so whole and uncomplicated. He was open and strong, every part of him representing the normality that she longed for but wondered whether she would ever find for herself.

During the four months that she had known him, the trust that she had felt on that initial meeting had remained unaltered. The fact that it had neither dwindled nor grown stronger reaffirmed that her first instincts had been right. She *had* recognised it instantly. Here was a man, finally, whom she could rely on. He was not flinching from her in disgust as she drew back the curtains on the grim reality of her existence, but, if anything, curving nearer.

Although James was devastated by what she was saying, rocked with disappointment that the fairy-tale marriage which he too had wanted to believe in was finished, he knew immediately that she needed him; that if he registered the slightest flicker of doubt, he would lose her for ever. He knew that she needed help and that the best thing he could possibly do for her now was to let her talk.

Diana had no time to consider her relief, she was too busy dismantling the cobweb of lies that made up her life. Barely pausing for breath and too cautious to risk seeing the truth of James's reaction on his face, she kept her head down and, pulling at her hands, blurted everything out in an unstoppable rush.

She loved her sons beyond measure, she said, and the last thing that she ever wanted to do was to create another broken home. She had been so very unhappy as a little girl when her parents divorced, so lonely and afraid, she explained, that she had sworn to herself that she would never, ever inflict that level of suffering on a child of her own. The very fact that here she was, potentially doing exactly that to her dearest boys, was, she said, devastating. It was crucifying her.

As James listened, every pulse in his body straining to give her the attention she so clearly needed, Diana started to let go. She could feel his warmth towards her, like the first blast of humidity that hits you when you arrive in a hot destination. It was as if she was leaving the cold, artificial air of the aeroplane and stepping, momentarily blinded, into that rich golden light with its glinting promise of something different, something better. Something that she would be unlikely to forget.

'I am surrounded by people but so alone,' she said simply, and he knew that this cry for help, like the ghostly wail of a wounded animal, would haunt him for ever.

Then, she reached out and touched his hand. Holding his breath and scarcely moving his body so as not to alarm her, he gently, firmly, squeezed the hand that had found its way into his palm. Now they sat united in perfect silence, relieved that with this tiny gesture, which they both knew spoke volumes, the first step had been taken. His touch was like a promise and, at that moment, he could not possibly have known how deeply he would honour it.

'You are not alone,' he said softly; 'you have me.'

2

It never occurred to James to sit quietly and diligently examine the maelstrom of feelings that swirled around in his head. Of course, he was aware that he felt sad for Diana. Sad that she was dizzy with distress, and particularly sad with the sombre thought that her marriage was over and that all the hopes it had carried were smashed.

And he would have been lying to himself, had he not acknowledged the feeling of excitement that, when he allowed it to, filled his whole body. He was overwhelmed with delight that Diana, this woman he respected and loved, who was such an important figure in the world, wanted *him* to be of assistance. Wanted *him* to help her. No, more than that – wanted *him* to be a part of *her* life.

By focusing on these relatively simple surface thoughts and ignoring their momentous implications, he prevented himself from facing the fears that were strumming against his gut. Whenever the warning thud of worry banged against the back of his mind, he did his best to turn his attention elsewhere.

After all, the interminable peal of warning bells that was trying to shatter his concentration could be ignored, could it not? He had not for nothing acquired from his father the rather convenient habit of turning stone deaf to things that he would rather not hear, had he?

It was like climbing a mountain with your head down, staring only at the path a few yards ahead. For you knew that if you threw your gaze skywards to the summit, your heart would be filled with the sheer terror of the ascent and the enervating fear that you might not make it.

On the level that we all know everything, he knew that the

responsibility that he was taking on might swallow him up along with his good intentions. It was awesome. But just as he had been trained through riding to stamp out his fear, he also did not pause to consider the size of the hedge. He just jumped.

Anyway, he had been bred not to put his own feelings first; that would have been unpardonably greedy and rude. No, what was important in life was to consider the needs of those around you. He had been raised to be a gentleman, after all, and that meant 'ladies first'.

It was James's relationship with his mother that provided the template for his rapport with women. Shirley Hewitt had always been his bedrock, the guiding influence in his life.

A small, county woman who always wore good snaffled court shoes and a Hermès headscarf, she was born in an era when duty came before everything, especially your own dreams and desires. Her father, a dentist, was an extraordinarily strong and kind man. Self-educated and clever, he taught himself to play the piano, progressing to luxuriant concertos which added hours of pleasure to the family's otherwise frugal existence.

It was from him that Shirley gleaned her tremendous strength, storing up inner reserves of courage as the years went by. She knew what it was like to have little; the underlying strain of that has stayed with her all her life. It was as if, even when times were good, she could not throw off the straitjacket of concern that held her back, gradually and imperceptibly wearing down the corners of her valiant, fighting spirit.

Fortunately she inherited her father's solid business acumen and, with her excellent eye for a horse, built up a solid reputation running a successful riding stables from the house that they moved to in Devon. With her husband's military perfectionism, the stable yard was always in impeccable order, the tack in the tack room gleaming in its proper place; and everyone knew that no one in their family mounted a horse without wearing immaculately shiny hand-polished boots.

It never occurred to her not to put her family's needs before her own. An eminently kind woman, without a selfish thought in her head, she was reared never to voice her own misgivings, only to tackle the job in hand. Selflessly, she always put her husband and children first. If they needed something, they must have it, and if she had to go without in the process, so be it. The heartfelt pleasure she gained from seeing them happy, from watching her children grow up into such considerate, charming adults, was worth any sacrifice.

There was little doubt that while she loved her daughters, Caroline and Syra, with the protective intensity of a lioness fighting for her cubs, the undiluted love she felt for James was different. That their relationship was special went unspoken, but everybody knew. Perhaps she saw in him everything her husband could not be?

She was sensible enough to recognise that suffocating him would drive him away, whereas by giving him his freedom, by never demanding anything of him, she would keep him as close to her side as possible.

Theirs was the sort of rare ease that means you don't have to talk. If James came home overtired and irritable, she recognised it instantly. Immediately accommodating, she stayed out of his way, keeping her own counsel until he was ready to come to her. She knew of his propensity for long, moody silences and often felt in his presence that she had not really seen him for days. But that did not matter; she could rest assured that in his own time, he would be his old self again.

James was acutely aware of the level of her sacrifice. His gratitude and immense love for her were densely interwoven with thick strands of guilt. He might have rolled his eyes to heaven in disgust at the mere notion that he could possibly be considered a 'mummy's boy', but it was that guilt that kept the fragile wisps that tied him to her apron strings as strong and unyielding as nylon thread.

He accepted as normal the fairly formal level of communication between his parents. In their house, great shows of emotion were frowned upon, considered undignified, so he had no real indication that their marriage was disintegrating. Certainly neither of his parents would have dreamed of confiding in him. The show had to go on, with as brave and cheery a face as possible. Emotional dissection was merely dismissed

as vulgar and unnecessary. To show weakness was not even
a possibility. That would be to admit defeat.

He may have been vaguely aware that there was an increasing strain between them, but he was totally unprepared for the
announcement of their separation. He was stationed in France
at the time, riding six hours a day for the Army with the École
Nationale d'Équitation. He spent a happy year in a small house
near Saumur, at Fontevraud L'Abbaye – where, as he liked to
tell his friends, Richard the Lion Heart is buried. Returning
early that summer to snatch a quick holiday, he planned to
meet his sisters at Badminton, where he was taking a group of
French riders to give them a flavour of British equestrianism
at its best.

Almost as soon as he had greeted his sisters, they took him to
the Juliana's champagne tent where, characteristically without
any drama or fuss, they told him that their father had left their
mother.

Before he had time to register the shock, James rushed to his
mother. He was too fond of both his parents, too religiously fair,
to apportion any blame. All that mattered, all he knew, was that
his mother was hurting and, without any whys or wherefores,
he must ease the passage of her pain.

Although he was twenty-six and bravely telling himself that,
as he had left home, the situation really did not affect him as
much as it did his poor sisters who were still at home and more
intimately involved, his pain was greater than he would ever
care to admit.

He knew that his mother's heart was broken, that despite her
brave face and hardy exterior, a part of her was so numb that
she did not think she would ever regain the same intensity of
feeling. He also knew that his sisters were in despair and that
he, the new man of the house, had to be strong enough for all
of them.

He knew that the power had to come from him, for never in
his life had he seen his mother get angry. She was so devoutly
emotionally controlled that she had never once let the note
of hysteria sour her breath. Part of him wished, for her sake,
that she would reclaim her strength, that she would face her

husband and frighten them all with the sound of her voice; that she would scream and scream until all the frustration, all the hurt piled up through years of lack of appreciation, little slights, and his failure to touch her heart and make her feel young and feminine again, drained away from her.

James recognised that at least that level of anger would be healthy, would clear the channels of hope until finally she could forgive and breathe again. Sadly he knew, though, that in the stalwart manner that he loved so much, she would bite her lip and forge ahead until one day, he hoped, the memory of this betrayal would be so dim it would loosen its grip.

It was not that James did not have sympathy for his father, whom he thought such a tremendously good man. He did. It was just that because his father had left his mother, he considered that *she* needed his support. He never asked his father his reasons for leaving, and he never will. Too respectful of his father's judgement and unwilling to stir up the murky waters that represented his parents' emotional life, he simply accepted the decision.

If deep down he was feeling angry, he never acknowledged it. He reconciled himself to the degree of honour in his father's decision. James suspected that his father felt that if he continued to live with his mother he would destroy her.

Like Diana, privately James found his parents' separation indigestible. Of course he was aware somewhere in the deep recesses of his psyche, into which he preferred not to delve, that things between his mother and father had not been as they should have been for quite some time. If he stopped to think, he could see that they had been going through the motions of their lives together in a monitored, almost zombie-like, lifeless state.

They had worked efficiently in the riding stables, they had seemed to derive a sense of togetherness from formally discussing the news and the events of the day and they had continued to entertain with polished ease, both automatically slipping into their well-defined roles. But where was the spontaneity, what had happened to their capacity for joy? He could not remember the last time he had seen his parents flash each other those knowing looks that represent huge whooshes of unbridled love. When had his father last taken his mother in his arms and told her how lucky he was to have her, how special she was and how dearly he loved her?

James had found having friends over to dine reassuring. As he watched with pride the familiar sight of his father handing a guest a large gin and tonic, politely enquiring about yesterday's hunt or a shoot and, later, his mother placing the platter of pheasant on the sideboard for her husband to carve, he had been able to convince himself that this scene of cosy domesticity was for real. But if, instead of seeing only what he wanted to see, he had faced the reality earlier, he would have known that his mother's soul had gone off without her, in preparation for the emptiness of her husband's departure.

Long before John Hewitt left, Shirley had been feeling, no matter what she did, not quite substantial. Often she told herself that she was doing what she wanted to do – tending the horses, gardening, sitting in the sun shelling peas, accomplishing the tasks life had put before her – yet she could not understand why what had once seemed treasure in her hands had turned to dust.

Though not aware of the dangerous level of this disquiet, James knew that his mother was functioning but not feeling. Like a parent who wants to sit at a sick child's bedside and gently stroke away the furrows of pain creasing the infant brow, he wanted to wipe a cool flannel across his mother's anguished forehead. He found the sensation odd – scary.

For the first time in his life he was aware of his parents' fallibility. It was a hideous confirmation that their old age was approaching and that he was catching up in years when, suddenly, he had the power to cope, the power to help *them*. The recognition of this role-reversal – of a child parenting his parents – made James realise that the time had come for him to stand firm. He knew that he would always be responsible for his mother, this dear woman who had given him so much. He accepted this without question. It was a matter of honour and duty. Plain and simple as that.

However, he did not ignore the pain that he had witnessed, pain that he did not think he could ever bear to come close to again. He had grown up hoping that he would marry, as he dearly wanted to replicate his undoubtedly happy childhood for his own children. He had grown up under the firm tutelage of such rigid, honest parents that he had wholeheartedly believed in the eternity of the marriage vow.

The shock and disappointment that even *his* parents could not sustain such a union caused his faith to dissipate. Almost immediately he lost his trust in people and relationships. Marriage, which had beckoned as a rosy prize for good behaviour, which he had presumed would fall into his lap like a ripe peach when he was ready, suddenly seemed too frightening even to contemplate.

He closed the doors on his romantic imagination as all he now saw were potential betrayal and pain. The thought that he might ever be in a position to hurt a woman as he had seen his mother hurt was unthinkable.

No; from that moment on, commitment became the enemy. He would protect himself, he decided, by allowing no one in. That was the safest thing to do. That way no one could get hurt. Casual affairs would be fine, but he would keep well away from the pitfalls of emotional intimacy.

Or so he thought.

As soon as Diana returned to Kensington Palace she washed her face, wiping off the remnants of that latest batch of tears. Standing in her light, elegantly tiled bathroom, she stared searchingly at herself in the mirror, and saw the first glimmerings of hope.

Immediately she went to her bedroom and, sitting on the edge of her bed, telephoned James. The hour that they had been apart had given her time to reflect. This man, this opportunity, was too special, too important to miss.

She wanted to speed up the process, to bring him further

into her life as quickly as possible. That she needed him was now abundantly clear. It was so long since her heart had leapt with the anticipation of speaking to someone that, as she waited for him to answer the telephone, she realised that she had forgotten what it was like to feel like this.

In a few moments – but at last – there he was; his calm, evenly modulated tones so soothing, so familiar.

If Diana had stopped for a second, if she had really examined why she was so desperate for this man above all others, she would surely have understood instantly.

For not only in his voice but in his mannerisms is James Hewitt her husband's double. Like Prince Charles he speaks in a slow, steady drawl, his vowels stretched out in that antiquated fifties BBC way. His facial grimaces as he chews on a question are identical, and however ruffled he might feel, he too would never dream of displaying it. The nervous twiddling of his signet ring would be the only means by which James's disquiet, like Charles's, would gain expression.

On the other hand, unlike her husband, James seemed to share Diana's propensity for fun. Unlike her husband, he did not consider himself her intellectual superior and shut her out with long words and alien concepts. And she could not get over how he looked at her. That gaze of such kind, deep longing and delight, his eyebrow slightly arched as if he just could not believe how lucky he was to be with her. That thrilled her to the core, her exhilaration tainted only by pangs of sorrow as she reflected that her husband had never once looked at her like that.

Both James and Diana knew that their poignant touching of hands in the Officers' Mess had fused their friendship, fast drawing them close. From then on their conversations took a very different course. Although they were not, they spoke with the easy tongues of lovers who keep nothing in reserve.

Diana told him how happy he had made her that morning, how confident she felt that they would share so much together. It was as if, she said, he had come into her life straight from

the arms of God, to help her regain her strength. These
were sentiments that would be echoed again and again in
the numerous letters she was later to write to James. She
knew without a shadow of doubt that he was the sort of
man who could make her feel secure, who could help to stitch
up the wounds through which she leaked so much emotional
energy.

As he listened to the bubbling torrent of her words, James
was consumed with happiness and fear. He was overjoyed that
she genuinely thought he could help her, but in truth – a truth
that he would not have dared level in her direction – he was
sceptical about the course that he felt his life was inexorably
taking. He was so used to his bachelor existence, he felt so
safe meandering about unshackled, that he wondered how this
responsibility would affect him.

Diana was too needy of him, too greedy for the light that
she knew he could bring into her life, to give him time for
contemplation. Perhaps she suspected that to give him any
space might be too great a risk.

Instead she telephoned him daily for confirmation about
herself and her life. That summer of 1986 had been so harsh,
so very difficult to cope with. The battle to keep up the façade
of a healthy marriage had been going on for so long that even
Charles, who was so adamant that the veneer must not crack,
had shown signs of strain.

There had been the arrival of Sarah Ferguson on the royal
scene. At first Diana, who after all used to host dinners to
facilitate Prince Andrew and Sarah's courtship, had been
delighted at the prospect of another young woman's presence
in the royal household. Sarah, with her thigh-slapping strain
of familiarity, was never likely to be a kindred spirit, but
Diana had had high hopes for a mixture of friendship and
support.

In fact, instead of finding that the Duchess of York was content to bask in Diana's glow and allow her initial guidance and
advice to sow the seeds of a warm and permanent friendship, the
Princess of Wales was quickly – if unintentionally – undermined
by the ebullient Sarah.

For when it came to Charles's family, where by now Diana could do no right, Sarah could do no wrong. Far from a friend at court, Sarah became a living template against which the desperate Diana was frequently measured. She felt rejected and hurt and her self-esteem, which was already crashing about her ankles, merely slipped further until she was treading it deep into the ground.

Diana's frailty and weakness of spirit were merely exacerbated in the face of Sarah's robust sense of self. It was Sarah's easy rapport with the Queen, their almost immediate bonding, that cut Diana to the quick.

The difficulty was that none of the royal family, except perhaps Princess Margaret, understood Diana. Her frustration with the trenchant moral ethos of the monarchy, her desire to throw open the doors on the façade of perfect family life and allow gales of fresh air to blow away the archaic sham as she saw it, was more understandable to Princess Margaret who had had her own heart broken when, more than thirty years earlier, for the sake of protocol, she had not been permitted to marry the man she loved, divorcee Group Captain Peter Townsend.

The Queen in particular could not see what all the fuss was about, what Diana's problem was. She had been reared, and in turn had reared her children, to sacrifice all for duty. Personal feelings were just not allowed to surface and Diana, with her blatant misery and constant emotional self-examination, was an anathema to her.

The real problem was that Diana was a stranger in their midst. No one in the royal household knew how to cope with this truly regal beauty, this thoroughbred whose slender ankles often gave way when those around her were stomping stolidly on.

Diana had been just a girl when she came to them, a brave little thing who, with the natural progression of the years, was struggling to find self-expression as a woman. She was such a sensitive creature, so desperately crying out for encouragement and love, that the tight-lipped aloofness of the royals carved her up inside.

If she had had her husband's arm crooked firmly around her and the wisdom of his unblemished love to guide her, she felt sure that, perhaps faltering occasionally, she would have found her way. She would not have been driven to the despair that frequently sent her hurtling off course, dangerously out of control.

Looking back, Diana could see that she had known all along that it was not her whom her husband really loved. Of course at the time she had not faced the increasingly glaring reality of it. How could she have? She was young and infatuated and brimming over with the folly of youth.

Her parents' acrimonious divorce had done nothing to temper her wildly fertile romantic imagination. In fact, if anything it had poured fuel on the flames of her longing for the perfect marriage. It never occurred to her that when she married it would be anything other than for love and for life.

Unfortunately, the man who chose her to be his bride, who selected her to be the future Queen, who saw her as the perfect candidate for a working partner owing to her shy good looks and her clean, impeccable breeding, had a different view of marriage.

He was in the impossible position of loving an already married woman. At first that had seemed eminently sensible, so safe: it gave him plenty of time to attend to his duties and to his country, to which he had pledged his allegiance and was devoted. But as it became clear over the years that this woman, whom he loved utterly, who understood him so well, who encouraged him and never tried to outshine him, was revealing herself as his soul-mate, his own marriage came to seem like a cage. He knew that he had to be ensnared, that he had to marry, but he never realised, never, ever envisaged that he would tear hearts and lives to shreds in the process.

During her engagement Diana was aware of the influence of Camilla Parker-Bowles on her future husband's life but she felt sure that she could change that. She dispelled her doubts, telling herself that she would do everything in her power to ensure that her husband loved her and her alone. She did not pause to think that it was wrong that his love should be conditional on anything. She just determined to earn and win his sole affection.

Her intuition raised grave reservations before the wedding when, still, Camilla Parker-Bowles appeared to occupy all Charles's thoughts. As she did not know then the depth of their relationship and how enduring were the bonds of their union, she naïvely assumed that all would be well once she was Charles's wife. Too young and inexperienced to understand the complex forces of chemical attraction, she felt sure that she, with her soft, lithe beauty, her youth, her increasingly thin and perfect figure and her all-consuming love for her husband, would soon knock Mrs Parker-Bowles out of the picture.

If only someone wiser and more experienced had taken the time to *talk* to her. They would have shattered her dreams, perhaps, but at least she would have been prepared and would not have had to endure the slow, deadening brutality of her discovery through the first five years of her marriage.

Love is not like that, they could have told her. We do not love people for their perfection, for their seeming infallibility. We love them not only for their charm, but also for their blemishes. We love them precisely for those lines etched around their eyes which mark their pain. We love them not for their control but for their fallibility, their vulnerability contained in that bulge of flesh which, far from being unseemly, is so endearing, so much a part of the one who is loved.

But no one did tell her; in that sense she was alone. The world was waiting for her and for her wedding. Her family and friends, far from shielding her in the bosom of their concern, knew that a commitment had been made, a commitment to the country, a commitment to the world, and that she must honour it.

She was too swept up in the nation's euphoria, in the drama of the big day, to consider for a second the possibility that when she was alone, wrapped in her husband's arms, she would not feel at peace. After the years of longing for security, of craving for the anchoring nature of love, she presumed that now, finally, she would feel whole. This was the moment that she had been preparing herself for, that she had dreamed of at night in her dormitory at West Heath school.

On their honeymoon the shock was unbearable. It had never occurred to her, not even for a fleeting moment, that she would be unable to satisfy her husband sexually.

As he was her first lover, she was still swathed in the chiffon of her romantic imagination. She had envisaged that afterwards they would lie together as one, physically and spiritually. She had believed that every day, as their love grew, they would deepen their union as they extended the bounds of their physical discovery.

If she had known the truth then, she would have known that that was impossible, that she would always lie desperate and alone next to her husband, just as he would lie alone next to her.

For he had found his ultimate passion with another woman, and he too had to face the savage truth, the realisation that his married physical life would never be truly fulfilling, however hard he tried.

Diana's confusion during that honeymoon, as they cruised around the apparently idyllic, glassy Mediterranean, fizzed continuously in her head. She could not quite believe, just could not understand, the level of his physical rejection and, while she convinced herself that as they got to know each other things would gradually be ironed out, the seeds of her own destruction were being sown.

She was breathlessly in love with and infatuated by her husband. She admired him beyond measure for the strength of his commitment to his country, for his thoughtful, searching ways, for his potent physicality. In her innocence, there was nothing she would not have done to please him.

Over those first fragile years of marriage she tried everything. Her obsession with her appearance was fuelled by her heartfelt conviction that the more beautiful she became, the more he must be bound to fall truly in love with her. Surely it was only a matter of time.

That she was fêted by every magazine in the world, that she was the most popular cover girl, her beauty and style universally exalted, meant nothing. In fact it made things worse. That she was adored by the man in the street, who had never met her, while the one man she loved, who was supposed to be by her side physically and emotionally, seemed unable to touch her broke her heart.

Unable to face the depth of her misery, she struggled on, pitifully unaware that in her quest for physical perfection she was destroying both her body and her mind. As she lost her grip on the handles of reality, she lost sight of herself, of who she really was. All that mattered to her was that she be something to someone else, that she behave and look as she thought others wanted her to.

Unfortunately, the more glamorous she became, the further her insecurity deepened. For the more the world screamed for her, the more people stretched out their hands to be touched by her, the faster her husband pulled away.

He was accustomed to holding centre stage; the fact that his beautiful young wife, a woman whose value he had lost sight of, was unwittingly outshining him both threatened and annoyed him.

Rendered too insecure by the legacy of his own childhood, too needy for praise and encouragement of his own, he could not bring himself to stand back with pride and marvel at his wife. If he had been able to let his jealousy slide, he might have seen that she did not want the world at her feet – she only wanted him. Behind all her striving so hard in public, almost breathless with panic that she would not be liked, was a single motive: that *he* should praise and love her.

She did not want this level of attention, this adoration. All she wanted was for him to see her as she really was, a frightened young woman who yearned to be in his arms, who longed for him to cuddle and nurture her, for him to tell her how lovely she was, how cherished.

As the years progressed, she tried to excise her hurt through work. If she could not win his intimacy, she would win his approval through public endeavour and praise. She knew how important duty was to him.

Yet whatever she did seemed to be wrong. It was like jumping from an aeroplane, freefalling, wondering when the parachute would open – and then realising to your horror that it was probably never going to open at all.

She felt unutterably alone amid the stifling convention of his family, a family with whom, no matter how hard she tried, she just could not communicate. Worse than that, she was unable to communicate with her husband, who seemed so closed off and distant. That she now knew there was a part of him that she would never reach drove her reckless with desperation.

The world may have only seen the sunny smiles and sparkling charisma, but, in private, as her hurt and self-pity surged up into explosions of anger, her husband was a party to her rage. At times she was like a terrified, frenzied cat lashing out to relieve her pain.

These violent outbursts of frustration merely left her impotent and drained. They fell on deaf ears. If anything was likely to drive her husband away, to turn the corners of his mouth in disgust, it was these unruly displays of emotion. He had never witnessed such intensity of feeling so close at hand before, and it scared him to the point where he shut off.

Diana always spoke of her husband as a man with a problem, a man who harboured such deep difficulties that he allowed few people, and particularly not her, close enough to catch a glimpse of what was really going on. At first, she spent years trying to unearth his pain, trying to help him, hoping that the process of discovery would at last unite them as she felt they should be united.

The tragedy was that the more she tried to gain his attention, the further she alienated herself, thrusting him faster into the arms of Camilla. For Diana could not accept that she herself was part of the problem, that her husband was in love with somebody else and that the closer she, Diana, pushed herself to him, the more fervently he wished that the earth would swallow her up.

That summer, after five years of struggle, had been particularly draining. She had nothing in reserve, nothing to give, and it frightened her.

There had been an awful instant at a polo match where for a terrifying second she had thought that their secret was out.

She had been kissing Major Ronald Ferguson goodbye after what had seemed an intolerably long and boring day of automatic smiles. Prince Charles, who never approved of or felt comfortable with public displays of affection, had chided her, playfully scuffing her head with a quick 'Come now, that's enough'.

Again she had felt an uncontrollable surge of fury. How dare he pretend that he cares enough to tease me, to jostle me, she screamed in silence. It is too much that he acts it out in public when behind our lying doors we both know that he keeps his humour, his sense of fun, his little endearments for *her* – for Camilla.

That he had not touched her in so long and was now pretending in this light-hearted way that all was easy between them humiliated her beyond measure. She would show him, as she had shown him before. In her wounded state revenge came easily.

On a previous occasion she had wiped the smile off his face when he had kissed her after losing a polo game in front of the world's press by scornfully turning and wiping that cheap, ugly lie off her lips with the back of her right hand.

This time she merely kicked out at the Prince like a truculent child. Startled and staggered, his anger aroused, he threw her against the car and, as she leapt inside, he swiped the back of her neck. Afterwards, when she had let her own anger subside, she had a wry chuckle to herself that, when they had both realised that people were watching, they had, with strained smiles, attempted to set the incident into the context of a friendly, loving joke.

That the fractured state of their marriage was no joke they both knew. That same summer Charles had seen fit to return to England early from their family holiday in Majorca, embarrassing her in front of their host, King Juan Carlos, whom she liked and felt a great affinity with. As usual she was left to soothe the boys, to reassure them that all was well, that Papa had had to go home to work, that he loved them dearly and that they were still having a lovely time. Even the sun and the water, which usually comforted her and re-energised her, did little to mend her broken spirits.

She lay in Juan Carlos's Marivent Palace weak and sad, full of self-loathing. There must be something wrong with her, she reasoned, that he should always leave her for this other woman. Of course, she kept up as positive a public display as possible, but nothing could comfort her. The thrill of slicing through the turquoise waters in Juan Carlos's boat had lost its appeal. In fact the more beautiful the location, the more potentially romantic the scene, the more she suffered.

She knew that she bored her husband and that once you bored someone, you could not unbore them. It was like standing naked in front of them, consumed with self-consciousness and not knowing where you had put your clothes. There was nothing you could do, you were powerless. You just had to stand there, getting colder and colder and more and more self-conscious until you froze to death.

She knew that Charles preferred his old coterie of friends, that he felt eminently comfortable – able to be himself – with the irrepressibly bouncy Lady Dale Tryon, with Patti Palmer-Tomkinson, the Marchioness of Douro, Lady Susan Hussey, the Duchess of Westminster and the graceful beauty Lady Penny Romsey. A hearty set, they seemed so united, so sophisticated, so loyal to their Prince, that Diana felt lonely in their midst.

She suspected that they saw her as stupid, greedy and spoilt. How could they know that in one way she was jealous of them, jealous of their ability to bring a smile to her husband's lips, jealous of his obvious pleasure when he was with them, of his ease in their company? How could they know the real Diana when she barely knew herself? How could they know that behind her imperturbable public façade she was screaming out for attention and love, screaming until she thought that she would expire with the effort of wanting, needing, to be heard?

It was as if no one ever really listened to the sound of her voice, no one ever took the time to understand what she really felt and what she needed to say.

Until, that is, she met James Hewitt.

3

Diana was overwhelmed by a desire to see James ouside the formal confines that framed their time together during the riding lessons. She felt a need to see him alone, to make sure that it was not a mistake. It was as if she already had a deep knowledge of him, a knowledge that she had no idea how she had acquired, but that she knew she must pursue.

So she asked him to dinner at Kensington Palace.

James was delighted by the invitation. On the day itself he was buoyed up, chirpier than ever, dancing on a haze of anticipation. The morning passed efficiently for him as he threw his attention into his work, for once fully concentrating on the pedantic detail of paperwork. Then he was especially diligent in the tasks he most enjoyed, making sure all was in order in the stables, organising and training the new grooms.

He was particularly glad to ride out that day as it gave him the opportunity to sober down and collect his thoughts. He always felt calm when he was near his horse, relaxed by the pure, animal connection. His life seemed to be taking an extraordinary course, twisting out of his control and placing him in the hands of fate. He was too intrigued to fight it and, as it was not in his nature to question it, he willingly allowed himself to be led.

In a way he was glad to submit, for this was the first time in years, perhaps the first time ever, that he had felt really alive. For once his senses were truly awake, tingling with an intensity of feeling that he had not known they were capable of. Of course, he had always had an especially keen appreciation of nature: more than once the beauty of a light veil of autumn mist sweeping over Dartmoor had stopped him in his tracks and refreshed him spiritually, as had the spring splash of yellow in the field opposite his bedroom window when it was dancing with daffodils. But to feel as if your eyes were permanently open, running continuously over the surfaces of life missing nothing, was new and exciting to him.

For Diana, the day dragged interminably. Each time she checked her watch, the time of James's arrival seemed further away. She could not remember an afternoon seeming so long. Eventually, having dropped into the kitchen to see that all was in order – she wanted this to be a special dinner – she went to get ready.

As she lay in the bath, she thought of James – his strong physique, his height and those broad shoulders which he carried well and which gave him the physically nonchalant air of the loose-limbed and athletic, his thick auburn hair which swept up and back from his kind, sensitive face . . . But it was his eyes that attracted her most of all. They were often distant and meditative but always steady, their knowing gaze seeking to uncover her truth. She could not hide from him; it was as if he knew her, knew her secrets and her pain.

She must not, she told herself firmly, burden him with these tonight. Tonight she wanted him to sate her with romance. She wanted him, this man who seemed so expert at making women confident as to the force of their own femininity, to be dazzled by her, truly captivated. There was something about the ease with which he wore his own sexuality that made Diana want to flaunt hers.

And yet she was uncertain in that department, riddled with fears and insecurities. She knew that somewhere, lurking frightened and embarrassed, was a hungry capacity for sexuality, a need to feel a fulfilled and potent woman, but it had never been encouraged, never been tapped. She knew that it had lain inert and rejected throughout the five years of her marriage. It had never been gently teased, never been slowly awakened so that she might begin to feel free and whole.

She dressed with extra care, delicately applying make-up to

her face to give the impression she was wearing none. She wanted to enhance her radiance, rather than mask it.

James, as always, was exaggeratedly well-dressed. He put a high price on his appearance and could not bear everything not to be just right. He felt nervous if he did not have a vast pile of perfectly pressed Turnbull and Asser shirts with the cuffs ironed back in reserve, and few things irritated him more than scuffed, poorly polished shoes. In his book it was positively rude not to be immaculately turned out, an insult both to yourself and, particularly, to your host or hostess.

He turned into the long drive that flanks Kensington Gardens and leads to the inner sanctum of Kensington Palace feeling supremely confident. Dressed in grey flannels, a blazer and a discreetly wacky Hermès tie patterned with rows of tiny cavorting animals, he knew that Diana would be pleased, that she would approve.

He stopped at the police barrier and announced that it was Captain James Hewitt to see the Princess of Wales. His blue Renault estate was waved through. It all seemed so natural, so normal, that he did not stop to be impressed.

As soon as Diana heard the crunch of wheels on the thick gravel drive, she peered out of the window to check that it was him, then raced down the stairs to greet him. Lightly tanned, wearing a long, floaty skirt, Diana captivated James instantly with her soft elegance, her inimitable beauty.

That they were both thrilled to see each other there was no mistaking. Their stomachs churning in nervous apprehension, they could not take their eyes off each other, could not stop smiling.

Diana led him inside, down the long corridor hung with magnificent oils, through an inner hall and up the stairs to her sitting room. A busy room, it seemed redolent of her, reflecting the dichotomy of her upbringing.

Those who have lived, as she did as a teenager, among the vast dignified rooms of a stately home, feel at ease among the grandeur of ornate, lofty rooms. But they also know that they are just caretakers of this grandeur, that they belong to but one of a succession of generations passing between these prestigious walls, down these long echoing corridors and out into the parklands slumbering their centuries of peace. So they learn, as Diana learned at Althorp, the family's Northamptonshire seat to which they moved when she was fourteen, to settle not among the frigid gilt of the state rooms but in the cosy hub of the nursery.

Their lives splintered by formality, they relax and feel that they can breathe most freely not perched on fragile Louis Quinze chairs balancing a Crown Derby cup and saucer on their knees, but slumped in the welcoming arms of the familiar, unsophisticated nursery with its lumpy old faded chintz sofas and ill-matching assortment of functional furniture.

Diana's sitting room in Kensington Palace was really a continuation of the nursery. True, the yellow and blue frill that edged the blue curtains did at least match the yellow and blue floral wallpaper, but it was not a sophisticated room. Rather it reeked of cosy familiarity, with its two large striped sofas sprinkled with Laura Ashley and Eximious cushions, their chirpy embroidered slogans, such as 'If You Think Money Can't Buy Love You Don't Know Where to Shop', hinting at Diana's sense of fun. Walnut tables overflowed with her collection of Halcyon Days enamel boxes, their hand-painted messages and dates pinpointing particular occasions.

It may have trilled with femininity, with its bowls crammed with heavily scented roses and its delicate watercolours of ballerinas in graceful poses, but James felt immediately at home here. How could he fail to feel at peace, to feel at one with this room which contained so much of her and said so much about her? Clearly this was her sanctuary, where she felt secure and safe, and where she could relax.

Excitedly, explaining that she did not normally drink but that as this was a special occasion she would risk a glass, Diana handed James a bottle of champagne to open and then watched his steady hand as he filled up the two flutes she put before him.

She came and sat beside him on the sofa and they talked of nothing. Their chatter, they both knew, was irrelevant. It was the unspoken communication that excited them. Their apparently inconsequential, at times self-revelatory comments were important only in the light of their individual but united quests to discover each other's secrets. They both knew that they wanted to experience each other but that first this dinner was vital, an integral part of their mating game.

She spoke in a light-hearted way of her duties, turning the mundane into the comical, drawing James into her world so that they were soon sharing a stream of unstoppable giggles. They discussed the two-part television documentary *In Person, In Private, The Prince and Princess of Wales* that had been shown earlier that autumn, and Diana laughed and cringed over her appearances, asking James eagerly what he had thought.

She told him of the squally gust of wind that had nearly snapped her car door shut on her fingers on a visit to the Maritime Museum at Greenwich and how, if her detective Graham Smith had not caught the door, goodness knows what would have happened. Fortunately she had been wearing a pencil-slim claret-coloured suit, she explained; the perils of wearing the wrong attire for Britain's unpredictable weather were such that she could have landed up in a fine old mess.

Then she moved on, and together they dissected at length her recent state visit to the Middle East. As she watched James drinking his champagne with gusto, Diana joked that clearly he would not have done very well on that trip – he would have had difficulty surviving Oman, a 'dry' country where only orange juice flowed. She gaily regaled him with details of the banquet that the Amir of Qatar had thrown for Prince Charles's thirty-eighth birthday, explaining that usually women were not permitted to attend such functions but she and her lady-in-waiting, Anne Beckwith-Smith, had actually been invited to join the hundred white-robed Arab notables for the glittering occasion in the elegant Rayyan Palace in Doha.

As she spoke, James recalled seeing photographs of the event, and that he had looked with extra interest at her in her ice-blue silk and satin tapered evening dress slit to the knee.

She was glad, she said, that when Charles had kissed her after she had watched him play in a polo match near Muscat, the kiss had been censored by Omani television. But rather than draw

James into the murkier side of her trip, the tension and tears behind closed doors – for this was not the time – she hooted with laughter and relief that she had never once been presented with the traditional whole sheep complete with bulging eyes to eat.

As he listened, James took her hand and, lightly caressing it, looked deep into her eyes. They were so beautiful, so warm and blue, he thought – but so broken in their expression.

He looked over her soft creamy hands, and the sight of her closely bitten nails distressed him. It was enough that he knew of her inner torment, that he could sense the surges of anguish she was trying to hide; he hated to see such raw, ugly displays of it.

Diana playfully snatched her hand away and laughingly admitted that this was a habit she could not yet break. With teasing severity she chided him, telling him off for being so critical, but inwardly her heart was dancing. He *cared*.

They were at that perilous stage where they needed to touch each other; mere talk was no longer enough. For now they could be only partly appeased, would have to be satisfied with tender jostling, with the wipe of a palm over the back of a hand, with an elbow roguishly tickling a rib to make a point. As they sat side by side on the sofa, the hair's breadth between them seemed as wide as an ocean, yet they were intimately aware of each other and of how close they actually were.

Their bodies were electric, aching to embrace, yet the anticipation, the fervour of expectation, was almost more delicious. It was as if they both agreed that the split second before you kiss, when you know that it is going to happen but at the same time are not quite sure, is a moment of ecstasy that can never be repeated and is worth holding on to for as long as is humanly possible.

The footman entered and quietly announced dinner.

Diana led James through an ante-room containing a grand piano scattered with photographs in silver frames and on into the dining room. Straight-backed, his head cocked to one side in appreciation and awe, James took in the majestic paintings lining the walls. He adored the huge military oils, the tremendous battle scenes, the frantic, vivid Turners which outshone anything he had ever seen in the National Gallery or the Tate.

As Diana beckoned him to his chair at the round table which could seat twelve, he noted the simple elegance of the setting: the gleaming silver candlesticks reflected in the polished wood, the sparkle of crystal glasses, the heavy starched linen napkins, and the scent of his favourite arum lilies wafting from a tall vase on the sideboard.

Diana said that she would not drink any more, that she was already feeling slightly tipsy so she would just have water, but that he must help himself to wine. She had instructed the staff to leave them alone and she served James from a hotplate on the sideboard. She took undisguised pleasure in carefully arranging his plate with paper-thin slices of rare roast beef, new potatoes and baby carrots and putting it before him, grazing his shoulder affectionately with her hand as she did so.

Unlike Diana, James ate and drank heartily. It never occurred to him not to. He had been brought up to appreciate good food and wine, uninhibited by any dietary consciousness. Unlike Diana he had never felt guilty after eating too much or guzzling a rich pudding. He had never considered calorific content to be even remotely important. It was a newfangled concept, an emblem of an era that was alien to him. He was a straightforward meat, potatoes and vegetable man. He endured salad only if it was smothered in mayonnaise, and would eat his apple crumble drenched with double cream and then have a second helping. He thought nothing of drinking a bottle of good claret and then, after a few ports, turning to the serious business of a long whisky-soaked night.

Diana, tormented as she was by a fear of food, a love-hate relationship which was slowly destroying her, marvelled at James's capacity for food, for drink and for life. She admired the way he could sate himself, never fearing the consequences of excess, the way he could leave the table satisfied, nourished, and then gaily toss a few chocolates into his mouth with coffee without giving it a second thought.

She may not have realised it then, but what she actually

admired, and indeed envied, was his normality, his healthy energy, completely devoid of obsession. Not for him the guilt-ridden, anxious awareness of precisely when and what and how much he ate. He thought of food only when pangs of hunger prompted him to look at his watch and register how long it was until lunch.

Diana seemed to get a perverse pleasure from giving him a large triangle of apple tart and herself a small sliver. She looked relieved as she watched him submerge his portion in cream because that meant that she would not have to eat so much. It was as if someone else's consumption of what she considered vast quantities vindicated her, let her off the hook. It ensured that they sucked the calories in their direction, leaving her free and untainted.

Of course James was totally oblivious of the demons in her head, of the devious games that her mind was playing. He might have noticed peripherally that she was a finnicky eater but, if so, she seemed no more careful than most women. After all, she had not got that marvellous figure for nothing, had she? And anyway, he hated it when women let themselves go, did not make the most of themselves. It was so careless, such a waste.

As he watched her he had no idea that maintaining that studied air of normality was eating up almost all her will-power. He was concentrating only on her face and her beauty which overwhelmed him. Never had she seemed more dazzling, more alive. Tonight there was no unhappiness clouding her face. Diana was at her most magical, her most sexual.

It felt good to flirt, she decided, as she flicked him knowing, suggestive looks, peered up alluringly from under her eyelashes and threw her head back as she reflected on a comment, slowly, sensuously stroking her elegant neck as she looked at him. James watched, electrified. Never had he felt such a magnetic pull. The room was alive with her, with her soaring charisma and with her devastating combination of dominance and passivity.

As the claret smoothed his edges, he reflected that this unforgettable evening was bathed in a surreal glow. Listening to her talk, of what he knew not, he could feel only the powerful connection between them, the current running wild and unearthed. He stared at her with his slow, full gaze, acutely aware of his own desirability, from time to time flashing the broad, careless smile that he knew she found so attractive.

Part of his mind strayed, fretted. He knew that she wanted him, that she was paving the way for him to take control, but how could he come to her? How could he cross the barriers? The transition from loving friends to friendly lovers was difficult enough in any circumstances – but here, now, with Diana? Diana a married woman? Diana the Princess of Wales?

His objectivity brought him back to reality. You bloody fool, laughed his rationality, don't be so ridiculous. You and the Princess of Wales, it is unthinkable, out of the question. You are just friends: good, loving, trusting friends. That is the sum of it and that is the only way it can be. As this sank into his consciousness, part of him was relieved. Disappointed maybe, but – he thought again – yes, definitely relieved.

Diana led him back into the sitting room for coffee. James sat in the corner of the sofa nearest to the fireplace and watched as Diana, perching opposite, poured his coffee. As she handed him his cup she let her fingers mingle momentarily with his and he felt a voluptuous thrill shoot up his arms. Diana, fully aware of and exhilarated by the effect that she was having on him, had never been more confident.

Equally she was rapt, absorbed by his calm, easy masculinity. All she knew was that she ached to be in his arms, to feel secure, protected by his strength. She knew that he would do nothing to dominate her overtly yet would dominate her completely, absolving her of all responsibility from the instant she was with him.

Suddenly, she could not bear it any longer. Her need was too much, she was starting to flail. So, with the ease of a dancer performing a well-worn routine, she stood up, walked across to him and slipped sideways on to his lap.

As she landed on him, cupping her hands behind his neck, Jame was both raging with desire and taken by surprise. That she should come to him so directly, without any further flirtatious ambiguity, seemed unbelievable. Yet, with his antennae on full alert, he was aware of her yearning, of her deep need to be held, to feel supported. As he took her in his arms and held her, it was as if he was infusing her body with a desperately longed-for elixir of love and strength.

He kissed her tenderly, romantically. He was hungry for her but suspected that this soft nurturing was all that she wanted, all that she expected.

He was unaware that what she needed, what she really wanted, was passion. To be made to feel whole. To be made to feel proud of her sexuality. To be made to regain confidence in herself as a woman. He did not know yet that she was still reeling with hurt from her husband's lack of desire for her, that inside she felt barren, ugly and unfeminine, that she had spent hours lying in bed at night dissecting her body, endlessly enumerating to herself its deficiencies, telling herself that she was not good enough, that she was lacking.

She was to confess to James on a later occasion that she had felt separated from most women, as if they were members of a secret club to which she did not belong, and which she did not have the skills or experience to join.

She was determined that now she was going to change all that. The time was right, the man had come. She was going to allow herself to be loved, to be covered in warmth. And here was this quiet, proficient man, brave enough to meet the challenge. Every step she had taken towards him he had calmly met. There were no questions, no doubts, no anxious twitterings, no double bluffs or shying away, merely strong, uncomplicated steps towards her.

Diana stood up and without saying a word stretched out her hand and slowly led James to her bedroom.

Later she lay in his arms and wept. She wept for all the times she had been left feeling deficient and alone, and the times when she had longed for such a union to melt her into her husband's bones as she had melted so softly into James's.

She wept for all the times she had been left confused and

dissatisfied, yearning for what then she did not know – while knowing that there was more – but now knew. For the agony of the times she had lain beside her husband feeling utterly shut out, alienated and dismissed, while now she lay accepted, cherished and as one.

And she wept bitterly for the part of her that had died with Charles's rejection, that delicate bud of youthful optimism and confidence which had been ripped cruelly from its stem before it had had time to open.

She wept with fear that that part of her would never be rediscovered, that it was too late for her to shake off the self-consciousness with which his rejection had coated her. Would she ever learn to forget herself, to forget her body and lose herself in the moment? Could she learn to give herself up?

James did not speak, did not question the source of the tears that dripped down her face. He suspected that he knew their origin, and it saddened him. He lay still, not allowing the force that he was holding her with to waver for a second. His quiet, calm, undemanding support enwrapped her like a warm coat in winter.

He knew that there was no going back now, no room for doubt. The second the rapid vibrations had coursed through his blood, he had become a part of her. He knew now that as long as she needed him, as long as he could help her, he would stay by her side.

He suspected that it would be a long process, so deep was her hurt. But he had time and he had patience and he loved her. As he looked at her, so soft and vulnerable in his arms, he felt a profound happiness and knew that he would do whatever it took to give her the support to let her fall apart and the strength and self-belief to enable her to put herself together again.

They both knew that she was crying not just from pain but from pleasure, crying with the deliriously happy realisation that finally it had been as she knew it could be, knew it should have been.

As she lay next to him, with his muscular arm wrapped tight around her, she marvelled at his uncomplicated masculinity.

He was blessed with a potent physical candour, a belief in his own body which amazed her. He was so natural in his nakedness. Unlike Diana, he had never thought of questioning his physical self. It was not in his background or his bearing. He had never allowed himself the luxury of obsessive self-examination. A body was a body; it was simple as that, and nothing to fuss over.

But it's true, nevertheless, that he was quite pleased with his torso, that he did take a certain pride in his tall, athletic frame. He knew that he could walk naked across a room, secure in the knowledge that all was as it should be.

When Diana looked in the mirror, even if deep down she could assure herself that really everything was fine, all she saw were imagined deficiences. The world may have raved about her splendid figure, but how could she believe it, how could she possibly be so perfect if her husband had turned his back on her? Her self-esteem had been destroyed by negativity and doubt, her self-vision was dangerously out of focus. On desperate days, when her self-loathing reached a hideous crescendo, it was as if she was looking in a fairground mirror and all she could see was ugliness. Then she could not console herself, and she tortured herself for her inadequacies; no wonder she was rejected, no wonder her husband preferred to be in the arms of another woman.

Of course, James was for the moment completely unaware of the sick, twisted little games of her mind-play. All he saw was the reality of her beauty, the diaphanous glow of her tear-stained face, her glassy eyes, her long slender legs, which seemed almost childlike in their innocence, stretched out across the bed.

As he watched her and gently stroked wisps of her hair across and away from her forehead, he was overcome by the strength of his feeling, swept away by the vulnerability that lay unguarded in front of him.

They remained locked together in silence, in perfect communion. They had no need to talk, there would be plenty of time for that later. Instead they turned and looked at each other with a deep, serious gaze, their eyes full of tender happiness and a measure of disbelief as they searched each other for any signs of regret.

There were none. Diana might have felt slightly shy, with flickers of inhibition threatening to close her off. After all, she had revealed herself to him so completely, had travelled with him to where she had never been before. But, she asked herself, what need had she to turn from him now? It had all seemed so natural, so effortlessly right; and he had been so kind, so supportive.

For the first time in her adult life, as she lay protected and comforted by this man, she felt at peace, as if she had come home after years stranded in an empty windswept plain. For once she was not going to spoil the perfection of the moment with her gnawing petty fears. If she was mature enough to invite the situation, she had to learn to cope with it. She had to learn to let herself be.

As he lay in her bed, a bed that at least he could reassure himself Prince Charles did not sleep in as they had separate bedrooms, with Diana protected in his arms sleeping the dead sleep of the exhausted, James reflected that it had never been like this for him before. He studied her sleeping, so pretty and defenceless, her soft face squashing into him, and he was filled with warm, passionate emotion. He could feel the gentle movements of her breathing against his chest and was quite overcome by the beauty and peace of the scene.

In the dusky light, he had time to survey the room. He was struck by the childlike essence of her, as if part of her had never grown up, could not forget the romantic dreams of her childhood. The maturity of her big, double bed was undermined by the sofa at the end of it on which lay, in a neat line, about thirty cuddly animals – animals that had been with her in her childhood, which she had tucked up in her bed at Park House and which had comforted her and represented a certain security which she was not about to, was not ready to, desert.

Later he would tease her endlessly about those soft toys, throwing them with gay abandon about the room. But she was ready for that by then, was ready to see them flung across the thick cream carpet or gently hurled at the lightly patterned walls hung with elegant oils.

He lay wide awake, too exhilarated to sleep, savouring every second of their union. That it had seemed so natural delighted him. He found it hard to believe, but he felt as if finally his splintered soul had met its other half and become one. In the past he had always felt a stirring, a need to pull away, to be alone, and the knowledge that he had to stay or feelings would be hurt had invariably filled him with a mild claustrophobia.

But now it was different. He felt a new freedom, a liberation such as never before. He wondered how he would ever bring himself to depart. Now, it would be like ripping part of himself away and leaving it behind, knowing that he would ache with a deep sense of loss until he was complete again.

Hearing the chiming of the clock outside, he wondered when he should go. He listened as the hours ticked away and as the clock struck two in the morning, he decided that he should leave. He could not risk letting go completely, falling deep into her and mingling with her sleep; he might be found in the morning. Gently he disentangled Diana from him and slipped into her bathroom to dress. He looked around, peering at the many photographs of her boys, William and Harry, the frames crowding round her basin and lining the edge of the expansive bath. It was not an opulent room, but it was light, spacious and fragrant with its mirrored walls and expensive-smelling soaps.

He quickly became aware of a glaring omission: that among the gay, happy family photographs in this fresh sanctuary of hers, there was not a single picture of her husband.

He crept next door and sat on the edge of the bed, softly caressing her, lightly kissing her awake so that he could talk to her.

She said that she could not bear the thought of his going, that her bed would seem intolerably cold and lonely without him now that it had tasted his warmth. As she clung to him, he told her that leaving her was a Herculean task, one of the most difficult things he had ever had to do, and that that would always be the case. But for her sake, and even for his own, he had to be strong and positive.

He said that they were so lucky to have found each other, to have come together in this magical way, and that this evening would be etched into him for ever. Whatever happened, nobody could take away what they had shared. He promised her that whatever it took, he would make her happy because he knew that he could, knew that he should; they could not deny the ease with which they fitted together, mentally and physically.

Diana needed reassurance and the strength of his commitment, so great was her fear of abandonment, and he knew this. So he soothed away her insecurities with words of love and encouragement. He told her just how beautiful she was. Had she any idea how special she was? He said that she made his heart sing.

And again she asked him whether she was attractive enough, sexual enough. Her underlying fears that she was not good enough bubbled over in her anguish at the impending separation. He took her hand and told her the truth. In his deep, measured voice he said gravely, 'Diana, you have no reason to fret so, to tear yourself apart. You are an exceptionally beautiful, eminently capable, loving woman. Of course I find you attractive. Of course I am aroused by you. I love you.' And then he left.

He nipped lightly down the stairs and out into the night. He hardly noticed the cool, brisk air that greeted him; it had no power to dim his electric glow. He was flying high; nothing would bring him down to reality just yet.

Fortunately he had trained himself never to allow a flicker of emotion to cross his face, so the policeman who discreetly nodded him back through the barrier had no idea that he was riding the crest of euphoria, that he was anyone other than a guest leaving after a late dinner.

He did not notice the short drive back to his South Kensington flat, parking the car, or even his ascent to bed. He was too full of her, his mind trying to capture and relive each moment while reeling in disbelief. That he could finally be in love with such a woman, and that he was sure that a measure of it was reciprocated, made him giddy. He lay flat on his back in his bed, not noticing the chill of the sheets, his body still warm with the feel of her, the muscles in his arms still carrying the imprint of her, where he had held her so long and so tight.

He thought that sleep would never come. He was so wide awake, every nerve-ending tingling with the memory of her, that he almost wanted to stay awake to preserve the evening in his senses for ever. But part of him was so relieved that he had been right that he also felt weary. He had not mistaken the force of their attraction at that fateful drinks party, and now it was being confirmed.

Over the last few years, he had begun to wonder, to worry; the first seeds of doubt had planted themselves in his mind. Would he ever meet a woman he could love? Was he capable of such deep emotion? He knew that he wanted, and had experienced, passion, but would he ever truly love and respect a woman he desired with such intensity?

He had been so firm with himself, so adamant that emotional intimacy could lead only to tears. But like Diana he had started to feel incomplete, to feel the twinges of loneliness, and he had begun to wonder whether there was not more, whether there was not, after all, another way. Now, he realised that he had answered his own question.

4

Neither James nor Diana was haunted by any feeling of guilt, any inkling of regret, when they awoke the next morning. They both knew that what they had shared was so right, so pure, that it took on an edge of certainty in the confusion of this uncertain world.

As Diana lay, stretched out, she rewound the evening in her mind and played it back slowly, pausing over tender moments and replaying them again and again, her heart and body alive with the memory. She found that today, for the first time, she felt the first flickerings of real strength, as if the much-needed inner flame of hope had been rekindled. She knew that in allowing herself this union with James, in inviting him into her life and presenting him with the truth, she had embarked on what would doubtless be the long, long process of retrieving her power from her husband and his family.

What reason had she to feel guilty? It was not she who had strayed so long ago, not she who had slammed the door on her physical married life. And when she had complained that the pain was unbearable, that the betrayal had scarred her, what comfort had she got? Who, in that family, had even attempted to show her any sympathy?

The Queen, as matriarch of that powerful clan, could surely have helped, could have at least tried to understand. But then, Diana told herself, she had to remember that her mother-in-law had been brought up in another world, in that country of hieroglyphics where the truth is frequently concealed. It is an airless, stultifying existence. Eyes choose not to see, ears choose not to hear.

Feet tiptoe down corridors, the full weight of their tread held back, so that they can waft away unheard and invisible. Then, if necessary, they can be deleted. It is a life built on the sham of rigid social customs, where men are entitled to 'lead their own way, do their own thing'. Worse, where it is almost expected that they will. Where it is expected that women will sweetly turn the other cheek, complicit with understanding, and, if they are really clever, if they are really up to scratch, will laugh mildly at their husbands' peccadilloes, at their really quite natural, quite endearing little traits, those unspoken extra needs, and welcome them back as if they had never been away.

Diana had been appalled by this, shocked by these anti-quated rituals which she had never envisaged that she, this optimistic, modern girl, would be expected to be a part of. Rather, she had married in good faith, dancing on the points of hope, to a man she had loved completely – and her faith had been destroyed.

Now, she was not sure that she was ready to trust enough for her faith in men – in life, even – to be restored, but at least as she lay there, the memory of James's body still lingering, she felt justified. She felt freer, newly able to breathe the clean air of truth, of honest emotion.

And, although she would not dare admit it to herself, the lilt in her heart also had its origin in the greedy, fleeting satisfaction of revenge.

While she knew that one cannot build firm, lasting happiness on foundations of pain, that she had webs of tangled emotions to unravel and great clods of misery to clear out, she decided that she was going to leave all that for a while. Right now she was hungry to enjoy her new freedom, longing to explore new heights.

For now, she was going to try to block out the dark and turn to the light. She was going to allow herself the much-needed luxury of being swept up in the exciting realisation that at last she was no longer alone; that, surrounded by people, she had managed to find a true friend and an attentive lover.

That morning, as soon as she knew that James would be at his desk, Diana telephoned him.

Afterwards, in the wake of their hour and a half's conversation, as James mulled lightly over the situation, again he found himself amazed. He had never felt like this before. Usually, he could cast women from his mind. Certainly he had never found a woman filling his every waking thought and accompanying him to sleep. Never before had he been so wrapped up in a woman, so conscious of her, monitoring her day as he went through his own, wondering what she was doing, how she was feeling.

Never had his heart lifted so when he heard the telephone ring and tensed in hope that it would be her. Never before had he relaxed so completely the second he heard her voice, the voice he had been waiting for.

Over the following months, their love affair gathered momentum. They spoke daily, often twice, enjoying long and involved conversations in which Diana would tell James details of her life, eager that he should share it with her.

What it seemed she most craved from him was his approval. It was not only that she hungered for personal acceptance, that she needed to be constantly reassured that she was a beautiful, sexual woman, to the point where James had repeated it so many times that he feared his words had lost their meaning. She also needed someone to voice some appreciation for her public life and duties.

She worked so hard, she explained, to please her husband and his family, and to try genuinely to help those whom she met, but she rarely got any encouragement, any positive indication that she was spreading any good.

James was startled by the depth of her insecurity and by the delicacy of her constitution, shocked that behind the impeccable public façade, the dazzling smile and the confident outstretched hand was this fragile creature tremulous with anxieties and layers of self-consciousness. He had had no idea that before every public engagement fear whipped a mass of frenzied butterflies around and around in her stomach until she thought that she would not be able to breathe with the panic. He discovered that the thought of public speaking filled her with abject dread, that she was haunted by the nightmarish terror that she would get to the podium, no words would come and she would be stranded mute, holding herself up to ridicule.

All this could have been avoided, he reflected, and it was so very, very sad. Instead of sinking into the quagmire of despair, she could have evolved, become replete and fulfilled, if only she had had her husband's appreciation behind her; if only he had occasionally told her what a perfectly splendid, absolutely invaluable job she was doing; if only he, instead of the media, had told her how exquisite she was, how loved and cherished.

But it was too late for all of that. What good were such reflections now? James could see that this was why he had come into her life, why he had been given this vital role to play – why he need feel no guilt, no shame. For, after all, by helping Diana, by keeping her on the straight and narrow, he was helping the country and the Crown.

His duty was to fill her with love and hope until she was brimming over with it, to help her forget her past unhappiness and to make her feel truly important, so vital and needed that she would eventually lose the self-doubt that dealt her such savage, debilitating blows.

He also knew that only he could restore her belief in her femininity. He could convince her in that area where she was so unsure. Slowly and gently he could persuade her that she was just as much a woman as the next, in fact she was better, that she gave off a unique and potent sexuality which he simply could not resist.

But these were not tasks for him, not orders to be carried out for the sake of duty. These were merely the unspoken rules of love, the language of adoration. He knew instinctively that, as long as he was able, he would work to alleviate her suffering, that every day that he could replace her pain with pleasure, he would do so. When you loved someone as dearly as he loved her, you could not separate their feelings from your own. Their laughter, their fears and their hurt became your own. In fact their hurt was worse than your own. You wanted to sweep it from them, to feel it doubly on their behalf, so that they would be spared.

So, daily, James welcomed the opportunity to listen intently to the minutiae of her life. She asked him if he approved of the clothes that she had worn for public engagements, and chided him good-naturedly when he tried to bluff his way out and finally had to admit that he could not remember. For James was not concerned with the surface of Diana. To focus on the seeming irrelevance of what she wore would be to diminish his feelings for her. He loved her too deeply for that. All he saw was the true Diana, her face radiant with beauty or clouded with sorrow. To him, she always looked glossy and gorgeous. In his eyes she could make no sartorial mistake.

Instead, what he really loved — where he felt he could be really useful — was listening to her read out the speeches she was preparing, helping her with her diction and building up her confidence. Then he felt he could put his critical faculties to good effect, gently telling her to slow down or to spread the timbre of her voice more evenly.

As well as the evenings spent alone in each other's company at Kensington Palace, which soon became the lifeline of their existence — if they were lucky and their schedules permitted, they could sneak a couple of hours a week there together — they continued to see each other during Diana's riding lessons.

Of course, by then, they both knew that she came not to ride, that riding was not really her sport, that she much preferred swimming and tennis, but that she came to see and be with James. Diana, who when she knew what she wanted could be almost ruthless in pursuit of it, had dispensed with Hazel West's company, enabling them to ride together alone.

Then, their behaviour had to revert to normal. But it thrilled them both to the quick to know that, behind the formal handshakes, the bowed heads and the frequent 'Ma'am's, they shared an intimacy such that if the onlooking soldiers — if anybody — had known of it they would have been blown apart.

And in James, Diana had found the perfect courtier. Really, he had been born in the wrong era; he was a man out of his time. He was entrenched in such a rigidly old-fashioned code of honour that, as long as he was by her side, he would never let a breath of scandal touch her.

She knew, without even having to ask him, that he would confide in no one; that their affair was so safe, firmly tucked away in his breast pocket, that it would never, ever surface when they were in the company of others; that James would never caress her with a knowing smile if it could be picked up on, interpreted; that he was so used to hiding his feelings that his face would never betray them.

The moves of adultery were just another code of behaviour that a man such as he, who lived by those rigid military rules, would learn to adhere to. Diana was confident that in addition to being such a very private man anyway, he was secure enough in himself never to be tempted to brag, his tongue loosened by alcohol in a chummy late-night session in the Officers' Mess. No, he was too controlled a man ever to let go, ever to lose sight of how much was at stake, of what was at hand.

And yet the risks they took were enormous. Of course they were always careful, their meetings planned with military precision, their approach to each other studiedly proper in front of others, but they knew that the hazards entailed in falling this deeply in love were bound to exact a hefty price from them sometime.

For the first months they pushed the future from their minds and dwelled only in the present, in the perfect, dreamlike seam where their happiness met. They longed for their rides in Hyde Park, when they would meet early and, as they walked slowly, their mounts side by side, could chat with subdued ease.

And when, in 1987, James was promoted to the rank of Major and stationed at Combermere Barracks, in the shadow of Windsor Castle, Diana simply followed him and they continued their rides in the elegant expanse of Windsor Great Park. There they felt freer, less conspicuous, as they headed off through the majestic parkland, gently cantering across that wise old terrain speckled with ancient oaks. Occasionally James would take off into a rich gallop, a showy flash of equestrianism, and as Diana watched this display of balance and power, she felt heady with desire and pride. She always felt especially attracted to him when he was dealing with his horses, admiring the ease of his communication and his fearless mastery of his beast. His was the kind of talent, a genuine skill, that often, she found, made a man more attractive. That James could swiftly turn from her and completely absorb himself in another passion was both vexing and yet intriguing.

Theirs was a true union, a genuine merging of body, spirit and mind. They had no need to smooth each other's edges for they could find no rough corners. Effortlessly, they fitted together. And just as James encouraged Diana, taking time to listen to her so as to understand her interests, to fuel her passionate belief in her charity work, so Diana believed in him. She was thrilled by his promotion, sending him innumerable cheering cards and letters to say so. She knew that with his kind, steady patience, his enthusiasm and diligence, his lack of fear, his belief in the military and his pride to be a part of it, he was a natural leader.

Because she loved him, she wanted to be a part of him and that meant embracing his military life. She knew how seriously he took it, how much it meant to him, so she asked him endless questions about his duties. She was eager to learn.

He told her that in his former position as Staff Captain of the Household Division he had been responsible for the management of the three Household Division stables and for the career management of all the Household Division grooms serving in other stables. He explained that he had been responsible for the public-duties roster, for briefing regular Army Assistance Units that came to London to carry out public duties and for the supervision of the Guards Division information team.

She was impressed when he told her that he had soon made

his mark on the Household Division stables, introducing a new scheme for recruiting grooms, and she could tell, from catching brief glimpses of his dealings with other officers, that he was extremely courteous and polite. He frequently chatted to his men, always enquiring about their lives and their news for those crucial few minutes which showed that he cared. So there was no doubt in her mind that he would fulfil his new position as a major tremendously well, that he would be respected because he would never forget his responsibilities to his men. After all, he never forgot his responsibilities to her.

James had met her sons, the young princes William and Harry, a couple of times when he had been to dine with Diana at Kensington Palace. Before they went to bed they would pop into her sitting room to say goodnight, often freshly bathed and cosy in sensible old-fashioned pyjamas and dressing gowns. These happy, family scenes impressed and delighted him. Traditional enough to approve of children only if they were respectful and well-behaved, James was not disappointed by the two boys – then aged just four and two – who were scrupulously polite. However, they did not suffer from the false formality that had governed Diana's and her husband Charles's childhoods. They did not hover in the doorway afraid to leave the guiding influence of Nanny's hand, or wonder uncertainly what to say, what to do.

If Diana had been determined to succeed beyond measure in just one quest in that royal household, if she had fought for the winds of change to blow through one area above all, it had been in the raising of her boys. And here, unlike in any other area, she had triumphed. William and Harry could not fail to doubt that they were loved, that every aspect of their well-being was carefully thought out and planned. As far as was humanly possible, Diana fought to ensure that her sons, while fully aware of their duties and the role that they would have to play, led as normal a life as possible.

They would bound into the sitting room like frisky young puppies, eager for their mother's approval and love. And while there were no limits to Diana's love for them, no grisly conditions or fobbings-off with promises that would never be kept, they were left in no uncertainty when they had pushed her too far. For she loved them enough to press on along the often arduous paths of discipline, to set boundaries which they might push and scream against but which, deep down, they were grateful for. For, Diana felt, if everything else falls apart, if life seems to be taking an unfamiliar direction, fair rules are at least rooted in certainty and represent the essential walls of security.

James could tell that Diana derived an almost physical pleasure from proximity to her children, that the constant bear hugs and showerings of kisses were mutually beneficial, that she needed pure, unconditional love as much as they did. It was as if, at the end of a difficult, careworn day, seeing her sons both grounded and reassured her – reassured her that, no matter what, she was fulfilling her role as a mother to the very best of her abilities. She only had to look at her well-mannered, sensitive sons with their tearaway sense of fun to know that she was succeeding. Whatever was going on behind closed doors, whatever currents of disharmony were running through the palace corridors in her direction, Diana could meet the trusting gaze of her sons and feel needed and indispensable. The very act of kissing a bleeding knee, soothing a hot-tempered furrowed brow or answering endless naïve questions gave her a vital sense of purpose, a feeling of moral solace.

Like most little boys, William and Harry dreamed of being soldiers, and they eagerly questioned James about his life. They felt immediately comfortable with James, who, demanding nothing of them, gave them just enough attention to arouse their interest. Not that he was uninterested in them, far from it, but he knew that to suffocate children with overfamiliarity was bound to turn them sullenly and shoulder-shruggingly away, and that if you gave them too much elastic, they would be tempted to pull it too far. He knew from his dealings with his own godchildren, whom he was fond of and got on enormously well with, that a short leash was best.

Perhaps, subconsciously, the boys liked having James around

because they were aware that he made their mother happy, that, far from the strained jollity they sometimes detected, her pleasure was real. James seemed to heighten her sense of fun and to ensure that she had a steady stream of smiles.

So they were delighted, tickled with excitement, when Diana told them that as a special treat, as a great favour, James had arranged for them to go on a guided tour of Combermere Barracks.

The day could not have been more successful, more special. To Diana's amazement, and to squeals of joy from William and Harry, James had arranged for two miniature flak jackets, two army-green pairs of trousers and two berets to be waiting to greet the boys. Then – accompanied by Diana, dressed for riding in her jodhpurs, boots, a pale pink shirt and a hacking jacket – in their very own uniforms, William and Harry were taken on a private tour of the barracks by James who, by now, had reached heroic status in the boys' minds.

They were shown all the different army vehicles, were taken to look at displays of guns and – the *pièce de résistance* – were allowed to go in a tank. Then they were escorted round the private quarters, given orange juice in the mess and introduced to several soldiers going about their duties. Laying on everything he could, James gave the boys a full taste of a day of real army life.

Diana watched in a haze of pride. She was bursting with appreciation that James had gone to this much trouble, that he had thought of everything, to please her sons. And she knew that he knew that in thrilling the boys he was thrilling her, and that touched her deeply. She loved to see him in his uniform, so suave and official, so firmly in control. It made her feel utterly feminine to know that James, effortlessly hosting this day, would soon take her in his arms again. It transfixed her with a bewitching tension, a tension she felt every time they met in public. It not only returned, but intensified each time until sometimes she feared that, if he did not reach out to her, did not touch her there and then, something inside her might snap under the strain.

The strength of feeling between them was escalating precisely because of these guidelines of control. That they could not see each other every day, that they had to hide their affection in public behind cold, formal words, meant that when they were alone together, safe in her Kensington Palace sitting room, they would let their passion rip. Both James's and Diana's feelings reached ecstatic heights as a result of this tension. Daily they felt as if their nerves were being stretched taut, that their eyes were opening wider and wider, and that the colours, shapes and smells of their existences were blossoming with an unaccustomed vividness.

James had such a keen sensitivity for Diana that he could detect the slightest change in her mood. Increasingly often, as the months passed, he saw a film of misery glide across her eyes and it distressed him deeply, stirring a sinking sensation deep within him. During the evenings that they spent together, and frequently on the telephone, Diana would reveal, little by little, the extent of her unhappiness.

She was twenty-six and locked in a loveless marriage. Worse, she told James, was the desperate, devastating loneliness: she felt that she could not tell her friends the full truth because they too wanted to believe in her and her fairy-tale marriage. The strain of keeping up appearances, of being everything to everyone, was exhausting her, wiping her out. Sometimes, she said, she did not know if she would have the strength to survive, or even if she wanted to survive.

At such times James would cloak her with soothing concern and quietly tell her that she had everything to live for, that she was a beautiful young woman, a fantastic mother and a gift to the country. No matter what the Palace did or did not say, he told her, she had only to look at the faces in the crowds who flocked to catch a glimpse of her, at the way patients in their hospital beds lit up when they saw her, momentarily forgetting their pain, to know how important and valued she was. She was a national treasure, he said, and he loved her.

When he was alone he would reflect on the shards of insecurity that scarred her, perniciously eroding her sense of self, and puzzle over where they came from, why they continued to haunt her so, threatening to destroy her altogether. He could not understand her violent mood swings, how she could be so happy and tranquil by his side and then, when he had to leave, allow the savage blackness to sweep over her and plunge her into abysmal despair.

When they were alone together, Diana felt safer and more cosseted than she had ever felt in her life. To have this kind, attentive man minister to her emotional and physical needs gave her a new sense of worth, a sense of self-belief that she thought had gone for ever. Being with James, she actually felt as if she had come home, not to a physical place but to an internal place, a place where she felt in one piece, where she was free of the demands of royal tradition and public duty and could be herself. It was a place where she felt the pristine, natural beat of life was as it should be, where she felt, at last, whole and at peace.

It was also a place of purity, a place that she did not want tainted with the ugly graffiti of her sickest secrets, of her most self-destructive deceits. So she took one of her biggest risks and decided to tell him the truth. If she told him the very least palatable truths about herself, then she would really know. If he was repelled, if he turned from her in disgust, then he was like the rest, and it really was as she had long suspected: she was unlovable and she would never get well.

Yet even as she risked the rejection she most feared and made her brave confession, there was a part of her that was screaming out for help. But it was not just that; her confession was the first admission that she had met someone she cared enough for, had found a situation that was worth being well for, worth fully embracing.

So, her head bowed low, haltingly and with difficulty, Diana told James that she was ill, that she had bulimia. At first her words had no impact, meant nothing. James had never heard of this disease; he had no idea what it was.

Sparing no detail, she told him everything, the unwelcome reality of the truth distorting her face with tears. She told him that just before her wedding day, her nerves had been so bad, she had been feeling so insecure, so lonely and unloved – unlovable, in fact – that, after she had eaten, she had made herself sick. It had come easily after that. Alone, for instance in the dead of night, she would eat more and more, cramming great mounds of food into her mouth, unable to relax until the table was bare and the bowls were wiped clean, and then she would get rid of it as fast as possible.

As she spoke those brave, honest words, James felt himself inwardly recoiling in horror. As he had never heard of such a thing, he could not embrace it and he was appalled, totally disgusted. So confident in his own body and with such a healthy, uncomplicated attitude to food, he could not comprehend this lack of control, this seemingly unmitigated greed.

Where he was so kind, where he was so faultless, was in his iron-willed refusal to allow the slightest tensing of a muscle or tightening of the corners of his mouth to betray his shock. While he was secretly revolted, he suppressed his feelings for her sake. He knew that she needed help and support, that this was serious and that he had to be there for her – that he had to be there for her *now*, not when he had managed to overcome his own dismay, but now. So, mustering strength, he took her in his arms and kissed her.

He kissed her deeply as if the touch of his tongue would heal her, as if what he was really saying was that it was all right, that nothing she told him would turn him away from her, that he loved her for her weaknesses as much as for her strengths, that together they would conquer it.

Diana put her head against his chest and sobbed, the moans so full of agony, coming from so deep within her, that James did not think he had ever heard such a tortured sound in his life. He was frightened by this level of pain, by the suffering that was in front of him, and yet he held her firm and steady.

'Let them come, my darling,' he said, 'let them come.' And she sobbed with relief and with fear: that she would never be normal, she would be tormented by food for ever, would always look around a table with greed and envy, knowing that, in public, unlike everybody else, she could only toy with food, must keep herself rigid or she might lose control; fear that as she watched other people calmly attend to their plates, she would always secretly be telling herself that after they had gone, then she could really begin.

She sobbed with fear that she would never be understood, and with relief that finally somebody cared. The relief that at last somebody was supporting her, despite knowing all this, knowing all there was to tell, was overwhelming. It was remarkable that, unlike Charles who had shivered with disgust, who would taunt her at the table, James was still by her side.

Of course James could not possibly understand the emotional and psychological bruising that went on, that the need to eat that food, no matter what it was, the need to eat custard before pheasant – the order did not matter – was so great, it was all-encompassing. The need was as strong as any addiction. Diana's mind could not rest until she had had her fix, had had that fleeting high as she gorged and then purged. And then, far from feeling relieved, emptied, she would be filled to the gills with guilt.

She sensed that if the physical stress to the body did not kill her, the guilt would. She felt a fraud in front of other people as she stood there apparently so pretty and immaculate when inside she was churned up by her own evil, by the force of her self-destruction. And far from looking at her increasingly emaciated frame with pride, she felt that her self-control was not enough, that she was not really thin enough, that all she could see in the mirror were great slabs of flesh, living reminders of her weakness, signs visible for all to see that she had failed. Then, the fear of her own insecurity would set her off again – only this time it would be worse.

Perhaps it was fortunate that James was unaware of quite the extent to which the demonic force of Diana's mind had gripped her rationality. Otherwise he would have felt powerless to help her. All he knew was that, calmly and sensibly, he would support her. So he endeavoured to learn about the disease. He discovered that it was a slimming disease that often had its roots in a traumatic childhood, in a perfectionist attitude to life that meant the sufferer never felt good enough and had a fear of growing up, a fear of giving up the reins of life and trusting it to guide you. Instead the bulimic had a desperate need to stay in control.

He suspected that in Diana it had been triggered by Charles's physical rejection which had shredded her confidence and destroyed her belief in herself. Every time she vomited she was ridding herself of great clouds of self-hate, but perhaps also she was vomiting up the disappointment, the loss of hope, that was poisoning her inside. It was as if she refused to digest it, refused to accept the rejection of her love for her husband.

Her relationship with James proved the turning point in this debilitating disease, for when she was with him, for the first time in five years, she felt safe enough and attractive enough not to want to be sick. And every time she carefully ate a plate of food, and every time she kept it down, she was filled with renewed hope. Then, she did not feel that she was a loathsome, unnatural creature, but felt normal, feminine, proud.

James never really understood her condition but he supported and encouraged her blindly. She told him that from the moment she knew that she was going to see him, she did not feel the need to be sick. It was as if she wanted to hold on to every moment of their time together, every shared experience. She knew how special it was, and she was secure enough not to feel the need to destroy it by vomiting it away, by destroying herself.

She tried to tell him what a terrifying illness it was, how ghastly and alone you felt, that you were only as sick as your secret and that her secret had been immense. It was as if she had carried it before the world like an invisible pregnancy – you carried it as you carried an unborn child, and you were aware of it always, submitting to every whim, to every unorthodox craving. You could deny it nothing. But instead of the pride of pregnancy, she told him, you were smothered in shame. Every beautiful sun-drenched day, every frost-bitten morning, your secret was with you, blinkering your view, and every time you laughed and suddenly forgot yourself, it whipped you back with a bleakly familiar feeling. No, you were not allowed to forget, there was no respite.

She thanked God that James had come into her life now, as

it had been getting so bad that she had almost feared for her survival. She told him that it was running her life, ruining it, and that she had been terrified last May that her secret was out. Did he remember when she had been touring Canada with Charles, how she had fainted in Vancouver and slipped to the ground beside her husband? And instead of sympathy, she said, her throat choked with sorrow, all she had met was his fury. All that concerned him was that her faddy dietary concerns might jeopardise her public duties. If she was going to faint, if she had to be so disgustingly self-indulgent, she must do so in private. No, Diana told James, her eyes ringed red from the never-ending tears, there had been no sympathy for her at the Pan Pacific Hotel overlooking Vancouver Bay where they were staying, no real help or support at all.

Trying to make light of the situation without diminishing it in any way, James said that if she was well only when she was with him, then they would simply have to see more of each other. She knew that he was just at the other end of a telephone, and he had bought a portable phone expressly so as to be more accessible to her. When she felt desperate, she must ring him. He was here, by her side, and he loved her deeply. He thought she was unutterably beautiful and nothing, absolutely nothing, was going to change that.

5

Diana felt that the full weight of responsibility she had been struggling to carry for herself was lifted once she had shared her secret with James. It was as if she was starting the slow, lengthy process of pulling back the curtains that had darkened her life, curtains that had been closed for so long that she would have to draw them open with the utmost care so as not to rip their fragile seams. To her delight and relief, it seemed that there really were good days, days when the cracks of light that were filtering into her life widened, and the more light she saw, the stronger she felt.

James was aware of this, and while he was relieved and pleased for her – and for himself – he soon found that the vastness of the responsibility that he had taken on was starting to hang heavy. He could not deny that on one level he was consumed with happiness, had tasted a manna he had never tasted before and never wanted to lose the taste of; yet as their affair progressed and Diana unburdened herself of her secrets, James's own secret got heavier and more difficult for him to ignore.

Although his whole inner life was absorbed by his passion, its outward course had to continue unaltered along its old accustomed lines. In order to ensure that his secret was safe, he had to carry on as normal so as not to raise suspicion. He had to keep up the façade of living like the young blade about town, and naturally he made every effort to be as social as usual. Yet the drinks parties and the boisterous dinners in fashionable restaurants held little appeal for him. He always felt not quite whole, as if a vital part of him was missing. He would search crowded rooms in vain, knowing they were empty to him because they did not contain her.

He could just about get through the odd weekend house party and enjoy himself since he loved the sport; a day's hunting or shooting would take his mind off himself as he experienced a form of oblivion. Riding came so naturally to him that he seemed to move without effort, as if his body was full of a life and consciousness of its own in which he played no part. Those moments replenished him and gave him strength.

But often, when he lay alone at night, waves of fear would wash over him and he would lie paralysed. That he was a soldier, a Life Guard, a squadron leader at Windsor, was a role he took very seriously, a role he felt proud to fulfil. And yet here he was, a loyal subject having an affair with the Princess of Wales, the wife of the future King. Then terror would take him over and he would feel desperate, helpless and alone.

He knew that even if he had had the strength to do so, he could not have left Diana, for rejection was the thing she feared most. And he could see that he was helping her. He could sense gradual changes, could sense that she was building strength, that her self-image was improving, that he made her genuinely happy. How could he deny her the happy time they spent together? And how could he walk away from a love that made him feel as if he had never really lived before, only existed?

When he really wanted to give himself up to worry, he would think of his own future. Marriage, which he had wanted, which he had felt he was coming round to as he saw his friends striding purposefully down aisles and standing proudly at fonts, now seemed to have slipped further away than ever. Of course, he continued to take girls out to dinner and to be as charming and flirtatious as ever, but his heart was not in it. He knew that these exercises were futile, because the place in his heart was taken.

James was all too aware that the love that bound him to Diana was not a momentary infatuation, not a blind flight of fancy that would pass and fade without trace. He knew that it was a grand passion, a hardy perennial which would probably last as long as he did.

In the initial stages of their relationship James knew that Diana, although wounded, still loved Charles and cherished dreams of their marriage working out, of her husband falling properly in love with her.

He had a great sense of her wanting to be sexually attractive to Charles, as though if her husband were only to catch a whiff of her new-found sexual confidence, he would be aroused by her as never before. Although James pushed such thoughts firmly aside as they were too insidious to contemplate, if he had really ferreted into his soul he would have seen that he felt slightly used, as if he was fulfilling a woman merely to help her realise her hope that she could fulfil another man.

He could see that Diana was desperate to keep her marriage alive, that she loved and admired Charles deeply and that she would try anything to win him. But the closer James drew to Diana, the more he could see that she was unlikely to succeed. It scared him that, as her efforts turned to dust, her love turned to hate. The more she tried to please Charles with the execution of her public duties and with her excellent mothering, and the more she was rebuffed, the more quickly her battered pride began to swell.

She was beginning to see clearly, to see that she had done her very best, that really she was not at fault, that she *was* lovable – after all, James loved her – and the stronger she became, the greater the sense of Charles's betrayal tore into her. It ripped out her whining self-pity and replaced it with deadly, ice-cold hatred. For you can only really hate when you have really loved, and Diana had really loved.

If James wondered whether he should leave Diana, the mere thought of it was so painful that he suppressed it, stuffing it down inside as he did with most emotional disquiet. He suspected much later that he probably should have, that in the long run it would have been the best thing to do, but the intensity of their love meant that when they were together, they were oblivious of everything else. From a distance he could see that his future was becoming increasingly complicated, but the moment he was with her, a feeling of such joyful pride swept over him that it negated all doubt. All that mattered was the moment of togetherness, when all anxieties and fears were obliterated by the purity of their love.

If he tried to express his misgivings softly to Diana, she tried her hardest to convince him that they had a future together. By this stage she so desperately wanted to believe in her own future, so badly needed to know that new avenues of life were opening up to her, that she spent a lot of time and energy visiting clairvoyants and psychics.

Astrologers told her that eventually she would be free – that she had a long tunnel of pain to crawl through, many problems to overcome, yet in the end she would do it. In a sense all that they did was confirm Diana's inner conviction that, however difficult her life was, however excruciating the sometimes breathtaking levels of suffering, her future was panning out as it should; that destiny was taking her firmly by the hand and leading her exactly where she needed to go.

James had little time for the psychic world. To him, a no-nonsense rationalist, it was all gobbledegook, but he would never have dreamed of shattering Diana's belief and her much-needed hopes. He felt that hope was all that she had to grab on to, and that without hope you have nothing; if these readings gave her hope, if they kept her alive, they were a good thing.

So when she returned and tried to persuade him that they had every reason to believe that they could have a future together, he wanted to believe it – he really did – but deep down he could not.

It was the same when they went to San Lorenzo, Diana's favourite lunching spot. He knew that she felt at home there, that she could relax amid the unsophisticated seventies décor of the Knightsbridge restaurant. It was so deliciously dated, with its pale yellow walls, its jungle of plants, its colourful pictures and paper menus stapled to raffia place-mats, that it demanded nothing of you. Going there felt as familiar and as unthreatening as returning to the nursery. And seeing Mara Berni, the Italian 'earth mother' who runs the restaurant with her husband Lorenzo, was as comforting as seeing your old nanny. She would show Diana and James to the furthest right-hand corner table, under the light, airy conservatory roof, and immediately order them a bubbling *bagna calda* with crisp, brightly-coloured crudités.

Later, when Diana had toyed with a lobster salad and James had demolished a mound of *spaghetti alle vongole* with its fat white clams, Mara would come and sit with them. The short cuddly Italian has a strong mothering instinct. She would take Diana's hands and, looking at them with her deep brown, owl-like eyes, speak in a low, discreet voice, her thick Italian accent oiling the soothing words that Diana longed to hear, words of hope which reassured her so. You are both going to be all right, she would say, holding James's tawny eyes with her mesmeric gaze. Then she would pat James's hand, saying, 'You are very good for her. You are so strong for her. She is such a lovely person and only you can tell her that. You can make her see. You have so much to give. You are such a good, wise man. Together you will share such happiness. You are good together.'

James was far too polite to let a shred of his cynicism show. He merely smiled, looking into Diana's eyes as she listened, rapt, to Mara's prophecies. Diana had, through her unhappiness, been forced off the bridge of life and into the abyss of the spiritual world, and she was increasingly embracing it because it gave her vital solace, replacing her inner loneliness with a growing sense of self. James might have been left on the bridge, peering down at her as she made her journey into this unknown realm, but he was not averse to her voyage. He might not have been conscious of it, might have scoffed if anyone had been so bold as to suggest it, but with his deep sensitivity and his growing belief that destiny was forcing his hand, he was actually ready to jump himself. Already, his toes were pointing in the right direction.

Although James recognised that there had to come a time in a man's life when the love he felt was so real that he had to trust where it was taking him, he was still unsure of himself. It was as if he knew that for a love to thrive it had to be transformative and, while most of him accepted that and welcomed it, there was a part of him that was afraid of such strident winds of change. He wondered whether he could, whether he should, pay the price for such intensity of feeling.

Would it not be easier to forsake these momentous highs and terrible, fretful lows for a more mundane, humdrum existence? Would it not be better for everyone concerned if he just changed direction, moved into a lower gear and continued his life on a duller but more even keel? Of course he knew that that would be simpler, but he could not cheat himself out of the knowledge that once you have experienced such passion, to walk away from it can only leave you feeling numb, half dead.

His mind swimming with these dilemmas, James drove to Cornwall to visit his father, John Hewitt. It was six months since he had begun his affair with Diana and he had not breathed a word to a soul, but the strain was starting to tell. He was worrying excessively and the constant nigglings, the background warning bells, were wearing him out. They were beginning to tarnish his usually healthy spirit.

Captain Hewitt lived discreetly in a small Cornish fishing village. Discreetly, because the woman he had fallen in love with, the woman he had left his wife for, was his wife's sister-in-law, Anna Courtney-Stamp. If James did not approve of such a union, he was far too polite to say so. That was not his place. Just as he cared deeply for his mother's happiness, he cared for his father's and, if his father was happy, he was prepared to suppress his own feelings and accept the status quo.

His father's house did not feel familiar to him and he would never be able to embrace it as his own home. He enjoyed visiting his father, though, as he admired and liked him greatly.

A captain in the Royal Marines, John Hewitt was a tall, handsome, distinguished-looking man. His life had been steeped in the military and particularly the Navy: his own father had been an admiral. His had been a rigid, formal childhood, devoid of much maternal love and nurturing home life as his mother had died of cancer when he was seven. Yet, within the parameters of tradition that defined his upbringing, John Hewitt had learned from his father the rare gift of communication which in a regimental context made him an excellent leader.

James had a good but formal relationship with his father. It was important for him to win paternal approval, and all his life he had striven to do so. He knew that his father placed a high priority on manners, and thus James's manners could never be faulted. Yet perhaps James could have let go a little, could have been a little more yielding where his father was concerned. Perhaps he could have risked showing a little more emotion.

As a boy, James, picking up on his father's polite formality, reciprocated by developing a similarly brittle veneer. As he grew older and realised that strength lies in the ability to drop your guard and let shafts of your vulnerability through, he began to regret the emotionless wall he had hidden himself behind. He thought of his father with deep affection, this kind man who had taught him to ride almost as soon as he could walk, this generous man who only ever wanted the best for his son, and he wished he could eradicate from his mind a particular episode from his youth.

His father had come to collect him from prep school, Norwood House in Somerset, and James, who did not know how to approach this man as he was so often away at sea that he rarely saw him, sat the whole journey back to their home in Devon in complete silence. Later, he reflected how deeply this must have affected his father, how much his introspection must have hurt him.

Yet it was not intentional. Though he could not express it, James loved his father and was desperately keen to please him. At Millfield, he strove hard to be recognised as a proficient sportsman. His father had been an Olympic pentathlete and James, more than anything, wanted to be as good as his father. He could not bear the thought that he might fail him in any way. As he was a late developer and did not shoot up in height until his late teens, he did not have the physical stature to be a good runner or swimmer, which was a source of bitter disappointment to him. Never mind that he was an excellent shot, that he fenced well, that he was one of the best equestrians in the school. Never mind that his father was immensely proud of him. All this, in James's overachieving mind, was not enough. He was not good enough.

Now, all he wanted was to go to his father, to talk to him man to man and to share his load. Although it might have seemed that James was closer to his mother, he actually found it easier to talk to his father, in the way that many English men find it easier to be themselves in their London clubs than in the comfort of their own homes.

He felt that if he did not get the advice and counsel of somebody whom he respected, he would burst, that carrying this secret on his own back was weakening it, weakening his judgement. He could not cope with the layers of confusion that were clouding his vision, and he knew that the only person who could help him see clearly now was his father. His father, who would have his best interests so very close to his heart, would set him straight.

As he drove through the winding Cornish lanes flanked by their thick, high protective banks, he started to feel safe. It was as if just the very process of going to seek help was already taking the pressure off him, as if he could be sure that whatever happened, he would not be so alone with his fate.

It was only he and his father for lunch, both of them sitting straight-backed and alert at the table. Over grilled *poussin* with vegetables and a good bottle of red wine, they discussed James's army career, his new position at Windsor and how his sisters were. It was polite, informative conversation, skimming over the surfaces but not really touching anything.

Over coffee, his heart in his throat and his voice tense with anticipation, James slowly told his father the real truth of his life. Pedantically, missing nothing, he told him how he had met the Princess of Wales at a party and had offered to help her regain her confidence at riding; how, as the lessons had continued, they had become closer and she had started to confide in him; how he had had no idea of the fractured state of her marriage and, when she had told him, had been shocked; how he had seen that Diana was in a great state, in terrible pain, and had tried to help her; how in reaching out to her, in aiming only to be of service, he had fallen deeply and irretrievably in love with her, as she had with him.

John Hewitt listened, letting James talk without interruption.

He was both touched and overwhelmed that his son should come to him like this, that he should be the first to know, yet he showed absolutely no emotion. Perhaps it was because James knew that his words would be met without panic, without hysteria, without intrusive questioning and most importantly without censure, that he was able to talk so freely.

The relief of letting it out, of sharing his secret, which was both joyous and unbearable, was enormous. The more he talked, the more he felt the constrictions of worry that had bound his chest so tight gradually loosen until, for the first time in a long time, he felt able to breathe freely again.

Looking at his father imploringly, he asked him if what he was doing was wrong, if he should put an end to it now, an end to his happiness – but also, to a great extent, to his pain.

Blandly, John Hewitt asked him how deep their feelings for each other were. What did the future hold? His brow furrowed, James said that he did not know what the future held, that he had simply no idea, but that all that he could attach importance to was that they were helplessly in love; that he was in love as he had never been before; that, while he knew that the outside world would be shocked, their private existence was enshrined in a purity which he could not expect anyone to understand. He said to his father that it might sound extraordinary, but when they were together, it was so natural, so normal, that he felt that this was what was meant to be.

John Hewitt felt for his son. While he was delighted that he had found such passion and that for once he was not denying his emotions but was actually playing them out, he was worried for his future, worried that he would get hurt. He saw immediately the position that James was in: that James would never have got involved in such a situation if he had not genuinely believed that he was doing some good, that he was helping such an important woman; that James, such a good, kind man, would never wittingly harm anybody and that in loving Diana, he was in danger of being deeply harmed himself.

Yet Captain Hewitt did not let his deepest reservations show on this occasion. He said that James was a grown man and should do what he considered best. Without the slightest hint of reprimand, he merely listened on. James, who knew that his father was sitting there completely calmly, that as he heard the story unfold was utterly devoid of judgement, felt a wave of gratitude. It was a feeling of appreciation that he knew there was no need to express, for they both recognised that in the strange tension of this moment they were bonding as never before.

Quietly, John Hewitt asked James if he was capable of giving Diana up. What did he think would happen if he did? James said that if his father really thought that he was doing wrong, that by helping this woman who had become so dependent on him, who needed him so, he was committing an unpardonable sin, then of course he would walk away. Yet he told him that he feared that course of action. He was afraid to lose her, afraid, he whispered, of the bleak future that would span out ahead of him which would surely be loveless and empty. But more than that, he was afraid for her, for he knew that Diana was in a deeply emotional, often unbalanced state, that after she had already been rejected by one man, to be turned from by another just as she had built up her trust would destroy her. Gravely, he told his father that he had never seen anyone so distraught, so churned up by life; that he really feared that she might even take her life if he tried to end their relationship now.

All that John Hewitt replied was that James must be careful not to get hurt. Then he elegantly changed the subject, and James knew that in that moment he had been granted his father's silent blessing and his support.

Diana was thrilled when James told her that he had been to see his father because he had had to confide in somebody, and that his father had understood. She sensed that the visit had done James a power of good. She had feared that his normal self-confidence was buckling and was greatly relieved that it seemed to have been restored to its rightful order.

As his old vigour for life was regenerated, their relationship took on a new pace. It was as if they had jumped the first hurdle and could relax, enjoying the gathering momentum of the smooth run ahead of them.

Diana had said that she would love to meet James's father, this man of whom he spoke with such respect and feeling. She felt full of gratitude to him for giving them his blessing, and in part she wanted to meet him so that her very presence could indicate her thanks. So Captain Hewitt came up to London with his two daughters, Caroline and Syra, to meet Diana, and it was agreed that he would take them all out to dinner. They would not go to a highly fashionable London restaurant – that might attract too much attention – but to a low-profile establishment in Fulham's Hollywood Road. The clientele at Jake's mainly comprised locals who found the restaurant dependable and jolly. Certainly the food was sound, if nothing more.

While her detectives sat upstairs at a table for two, Diana slipped downstairs to a private room to join the Hewitts. She was amused to note that she felt as eager to please Captain Hewitt as she had her father-in-law. That James's father and sisters like and approve of her was, by now, extremely important to her.

Everyone was on buoyant form and the evening passed without a hitch. Diana was dazzling – not that she tried to outshine everyone, far from it. It was just such a relief to feel so relaxed and accepted that she naturally let her delight show. It felt so normal to be among James's family, who, without the slightest hint of the fickle fawning of which she was so tired, were welcoming and friendly. Yet, like James, they all kept a polite distance which she appreciated as it gave her time to unfurl.

She felt proud to be sitting near James who, she knew, even without the touch of his hand, only those snatched, penetrating glances, was supporting her and willing her to win his family. He had had no doubt that she would, but it made him feel good to nurture the thought that they might love her as much as he did.

They barely noticed the food but, as usual, drank plenty. Even Diana managed a few glasses of wine and was flushed pink. Their conversation was general yet, with escalating teasing, soon became crackling and witty. James's sisters told Diana a bit about themselves, briefly running through their recent life histories in interview mode as people tend to on these first – often excruciating – meetings.

That night there were no awkward pauses, no stilted questions thrown into a den of sudden silence. It was so different, Diana reflected, from being with her husband's family where, their royalty aside, she always felt that she was on trial, a complete stranger in the midst of a family gathering, where, far from being accepted, all she felt was the harsh blowtorch of their critical eyes.

Seeing James's family, seeing how understated yet genuine they were, how much they clearly loved James, just made her love him more. She felt that they, although always respectful of one another and polite, spoke a language that she could relate to. They were traditional without being stuffy, formal yet relaxed and, far from being pompous, had a tremendous appetite for fun. It was all so easy, as their humour was her humour. Theirs was not the snide, intellectual arrogance that held others, less academic, up to ridicule; theirs was like hers, a good, kind sense of fun. It was more the jolly back-of-the-class humour, where you had to cup your hand over your mouth and, your eyes watering with glee, suppress great ricochets of giggles. There was nothing sneeringly sophisticated or clever about it.

During this time, the spring of 1987, Diana was possibly at her most confused and distraught. She was absolutely fixed on the maelstrom of her emotions and she knew that she needed a protracted period of self-absorption, that it was only by staring deep into the abyss of her despair, by accepting the dreary weight of her anxiety and examining it, that she would ever free herself.

When she was with James, she felt as if she had passed into a sort of dream world, an easy existence where she could be herself and start to build on the foundations of her new-found happiness. His mere presence absolved her from the conditions of actuality and allowed her the freedom to heal. When she was with him she took a childlike delight in being utterly supported by him, emotionally and physically, a woman clinging to her man. These were liberating times when she was able to forget about what people thought of her, to stop fretting about what the Palace or the press were or were not saying.

She realised that she was not yet fully healed as she sat and watched this man and felt envious that he could be so peaceful and self-sufficient while she felt so at sea. Often she felt as if she was perching on the doorstep of life peering in, an onlooker while everybody else – particularly James with his calm manner and solid self-esteem – was a participant. At such times she needed James, and even the rest of the world, to be aware of her; she hungered for attention and affection as never before, and she demanded it from James.

The very fact that she felt he relieved her of responsibility for herself meant that when he was not with her, her panic could grow worse than before. Sometimes her fear of coping with her own instabilities would grow so great, create such hysteria, that the only answer was to escape from herself. Then, she would frantically dial James's number, eager to hear him, anxious for him to calm her and restore her balance. If she could not rouse him on his mobile, she would ring the public telephone in Combermere Barracks and, disguising her voice with a muffler, ask for Major Hewitt. And soon he would be there, standing in the marble hall, his head tucked deep into the booth, his soft words diluting her panic.

The thrust of her distress was that she knew that she had to face the acrid reality that her marriage was truly over; that however hard she tried, it was to little avail. While she had long been aware of it, she had not wanted to accept it, to digest it. In her dream life, she had still had hope, but now her hope had been battered into submission, destroyed once and for all. She felt that she was imprisoned in her own unhappiness; the ability to take charge of her own destiny had finally slipped from her feeble grasp.

She realised that if she was to travel this lonely road without the love and support of her husband and the backing of his family, she had to have strength, had to find her own sense of self. Only then would she be able to retrieve her power, and stand up and fight for herself and her children. For she knew that her back was up against the palace walls, that if she did not rattle them with her determination, did not show them that she had an iron will, they would toss her aside and she would lose her hold – and that meant losing the most important thing of all, her necessary guiding influence over her sons.

James's support gave her the initial hope she needed, and his love gave her the happiness to fuel her growing resolve. She sought professional help, in particular from Dr Maurice Lipsedge, a specialist in eating disorders at Guy's Hospital in south-east London.

The discovery that she was not alone with her illness, that Lipsedge both understood her and had heard it all before, reassured her and strengthened her determination. She would ring James constantly with progress reports, sharing every illuminating detail that her sessions revealed. James was full of hope for her but his worries resumed as time went by and he could detect a pattern in her behaviour. For a few weeks she would feel better, exhilarated with new-found health, and then it was as if she had pushed herself too far too soon and suddenly her reserves were depleted. Then, she would sink back into what seemed a deeper trough than before.

Almost imperceptibly, though, despite her seesawing emotional state, she was gaining strength and with it her vibrant sense of fun was rekindled. It was on display when she and Prince Charles went skiing with the Duke and Duchess of York in the Swiss resort Klosters. Wearing the cricket sweater that James had lent her under her jacket, Diana playfully staged a mock fight with Sarah on the slopes in front of the press who were lined up for their morning photo call. While this soothed the world's fears that there was disharmony in the royal household and appeared to indicate that all was loving between Diana and Charles, beneath the surface the holiday was an ordeal for Diana.

Behind the chalet walls, she was the victim of her own volatile emotions. She rang James every evening to say how dreadfully she missed him. She told him that she had never felt so alone, that far from gaining much real friendship and support from Sarah, she felt further alienated in her presence. She knew that Charles felt comfortable with Sarah, that he admired her hearty zest for life; witnessing this simply made Diana crumble. It was as if Sarah's success merely sucked out the last of Diana's strength.

That Charles did not appear to want to spend any time with her, that when he wanted to go dancing he preferred to do so without her, increased Diana's sense of isolation, which in turn brought back great bouts of bulimia. Then the guilt and unruly self-hatred returned. As she retreated quickly into the black hole of her despair, it was not surprising that people found her irrational and difficult to be with.

It may have been half-hearted, but it was a bid to regain a measure of her own power when Diana visited a Klosters café with a medal pinned to her chest and told the press that she had awarded it to herself for services to her country because she knew that nobody else would.

When she told James about this later, he teased her that that was not strictly true, that she knew jolly well that he thought she deserved endless praise and that he gave her as much as he could. Perhaps it had been foolish, she agreed, but sometimes, she said, she felt that she was bursting with the need to tell the world how it really was – that she tried her very best and that all she got these days were stern, disapproving looks.

It had been just the same in Portugal, where she had gone on a visit with Charles before the skiing trip. He had been angered that she had allowed Prime Minister Cavaço Silva to kiss her hand. But Diana, feeling more confident with her sexuality since she had known James, was aware that the Prime Minister was captivated by her and she had decided to enjoy it, because it made her feel good – and it exacted a measure of revenge. How could Charles dare to scold her, to pretend that he cared when he was not interested anyway?

She returned from Klosters more determined than ever to beat the demons, but she felt she was fighting a losing battle. Aware that in her vulnerable state she was making poor choices and potentially damaging herself further, she knew that somehow she had to stop living in a shadow realm, operating on diminished levels far below her full capacity. She had to dig even deeper within herself.

James's devotion gave her confidence, but the more she felt it, the more she knew that it was not enough. It was as if he provided the reason, the trigger, and now she had to run the race herself. For no matter how much anybody loves you and wishes to remove your pain, only you can heal yourself. You can have all the support necessary but only you can take that first lonely step.

Diana knew that to rebuild her inner strength she needed more help, and she knew that she wanted to do it in a certain way. She could have gone to doctors and psychiatrists who might have sedated her and given her anti-depressants, but she wanted to *heal*. She did not want chemical treatment, a plaster stuck over a wound that was still weeping. She wanted, however painful and lengthy the process, to expose the wound and let nature – life – heal it.

So she began to seek alternative therapies, one treatment preparing her and leading her inexorably on to the next when she was ready. Over time, Stephen Twigg's therapeutic massage, Roderick Lane's hypnotherapy, Sue Beechey's aromatherapy and Oonagh Toffolo's acupuncture were to enable Diana to get in touch with her body and to accept it. Through their individual methods they taught her that unless she learned to love herself, to like and nurture herself on a deep inner level, it would be difficult for anyone else to. If she wanted to sustain a harmonious, permanent union, she had first to establish that union with herself.

These treatments helped her to integrate her mind and her body so that her mind no longer had the power to destroy her. Once she felt that she was in control rather than the victim of herself, she could build real confidence and strength. These various techniques rearranged her energy, shifting blocks of dead energy and affording her a new vitality. Gradually her physical and mental equilibrium began to be restored.

Of course, this process of healing was a long and arduous one that, once begun, would have to be worked at at different degrees for the rest of her life. She had both to heal the damage that she had done to herself through her bulimia and to learn to release her negative emotions:

guilt, fear, self-disgust and, most difficult and agonising of all, pain.

Sometimes, when she could not bear to cry any more, she would try to suppress her pain, to push it back down, because that seemed easier than facing it. For to hold on to the known, however bad it might seem, is less scary than relinquishing your burden and running blind into the unknown.

But she learned, as she got stronger, that holding on to old pain is more wearing in the long term than releasing it. She knew that she was stirring up muddy waters but she also knew that the sooner she faced the swirling maelstrom of her emotions, the sooner they would settle and she would be able to see clearly.

And, gradually, she learned the most difficult lesson of all: not to be so hard on herself; to close her eyes when they were self-critical; to seek the good within herself as opposed to focusing on the negative. As she lay on one hard couch or narrow, awkward massage bed after another and allowed herself the luxury of the attention she so badly needed, she learned to look after herself, to hear, in the healing silence, the timid whisper of her own inner voice. And she knew that the more she heeded it – the more she heeded the true demands of her body and her psyche – the stronger she would become. Eventually, she would not be relying on anybody else. She would be doing it for herself.

James Hewitt in uniform.

A marriage turns sour.

James and his sister Caroline at her wedding.

James (far left) and the Prince of Wales (third from right) on the polo field.

Diana demonstrating her proficiency in sign language at the Deaf and
Dumb Centre, Durham.

James standing on ceremony for the Queen.

Diana presenting James with the Captain and Subalterns Cup at Tidworth, watched by Prince William.

James in the Gulf in 1991.

6

As James drove through the Gloucestershire lanes, he felt happy as never before. In the light of the early-evening sun the countryside had rarely seemed softer or more beautiful. His car was alive with Pavarotti, the rich passion of the tenor's songs matching his own. James was on his way to spend the weekend with Diana at Highgrove.

That he was to spend a whole weekend with her, that they could stay the full course of long nights together, could wake up together, could sit on the edge of each other's baths and chat intimately as proper couples do, dispelled his past doubts. Now he felt that whatever sacrifices he had made or would have to make were worth it, worth this precious time when finally they could relax, let down their guards a little, be normal.

Diana was waiting for him in a faint delirium of nervous tension. She could not believe that she was to have him all to herself, to share this house with him, to show him another side of her, and of her life. It was almost too good to be true that she should be so spoilt, that she should have the three people she loved most, who meant more to her than anything, together under the same roof. Charles was away, and the fact that she was to have the boys and James for the weekend was surely a sign that in some way she was being rewarded. As she waited to hear the crunch of his car on the gravel outside, she decided that this was a hint of what life could, perhaps should, be like.

Soon James was swinging his Renault estate round the circular drive, its carefully cultivated wild-flower verges bursting with poppies and ox-eye daisies. As he got out, his black Labrador, Jester, bounded after him and rushed to greet

Diana almost as eagerly as his master did. The moment Diana
felt the touch of James's hand on her shoulder as he formally
kissed her on each cheek she felt relieved. Every time they met,
his mere touch resealed the trust that threatened to leak as the
by-product of every separation.

Excitedly she led him inside. She wanted him to feel at home
here. In fact she wanted his presence to enable her to rediscover
the joys of this house and its beautiful grounds. Lately, when
she had been here with Charles, or even on her own, she had
felt so ill at ease that she had become a stranger in her own
home. Then, feeling shut out from Charles and his love of this
house, she had nursed resentment towards her husband and
even Highgrove. If she had stopped for a second and asked
herself what was really going on, she would have realised
that she was not yet at home within herself; that she was
going through such change that wherever else she had been
she would have felt just as restless.

As the footman carried James's bags to his room, William
and Harry rushed to greet their mother's friend. They were
delighted to see him, and even more delighted to meet Jester
who was quite beside himself with all the excitement and
attention. In answer to William and Harry's pleas, James
promised that in the morning he would watch them ride,
teasingly telling them that soon they would be as good on
horseback as their mother.

Diana was positively jittery with glee. She could not remember when she had last felt so unreservedly happy, as she
watched James, so naturally playful, being so kind and so
interested in her sons. After a while, before things got too
boisterous, before nerves were stretched and bouncing bodies
overtired, the boys' nanny, Barbara Barnes, appeared and
hustled them off to bed.

As Diana took James up the wide staircase he was pleased
to find that Highgrove was not a pretentious house. It was
well-decorated in that expensive, understated mode, but it
did not feel much different from a lot of the country houses
of affluent friends he had visited. All the elements that such
houses had in common were there: the bottle of Hillsdown

mineral water and the glass that stood on the bedside table, the pretty tin of assorted biscuits and mints. Next to them lay the stack of mixed reading material: the ancient hardbacks, the well-leafed thrillers and the old, faded copies of *Tatler*, *Vogue* and *Harpers & Queen*. Vases of fresh flowers mingled with the Herend china on the dressing table; the headed writing paper with matching envelopes was laid out on the blotter on the desk.

As soon as James had closed the door on his claret-coloured bedroom, he took Diana in his arms and kissed her long and deeply. They both needed that intensity of touch to know that nothing had changed between them, to reassure themselves that, if anything, it was better. They lay on the four-poster bed, James stroking Diana's head and dotting her with kisses. By now they both knew that when they were together they relinquished all cares, lost their identities as they merged into one.

Those weekends, which thenceforth were to take place about once a month, always sped by in a sybaritic haze of abandonment. There were few sighs in their brief snatches of heaven. At night James would tread quietly along the corridor, three rooms from his own, to join Diana in her creamy bedroom. Then Diana would lose her interminable sense of isolation.

In the intimacy of her bedroom, safe in her four-poster bed, they slept the sound, light sleep of satiated lovers, asleep but always aware of each other.

Never did Diana feel calmer than when she awoke with James, both of them rousing at the same pace. Now she could almost bear his having to leave her bed early in case William or Harry should bound in; she knew that their separation would not be for long – soon she would see him fresh and correct at the breakfast table.

Diana would go down to breakfast first to be with William, Harry and Barbara Barnes and then, once James was dressed – always immaculate, totally *comme il faut* in appearance and manner – he would come down and enter the room full of morning cheer. Together they would run through the well-worn routine of hostess/guest *politesse*, smiling inwardly at their charade of 'Good morning's, 'Did you sleep well?'s, 'Oh, good!'s and 'Help yourself to breakfast from the side'.

Of course, Nanny Barbara Barnes was not to be fooled. Looking on with blank amusement she probably knew exactly why this handsome Guards officer came to stay so frequently when Diana was on her own without her husband, but never by look, word or deed would she have dreamed of registering her knowledge. That was not her place.

Once William and Harry had scampered away to the stables, James and Diana would usually sit for a while in a mood of perfect stillness. If he got up to get himself something more to eat, James might rest his hand on her shoulder as he passed or lightly kiss the back of her neck, but they did not need anything more. At last they had their most precious commodity, time.

During their days at Highgrove they were careful not to let William or Harry have so much as a glimpse of their secret. Quick kisses or caresses were sneaked only when they had ensured that they could not possibly be caught. Apart from the full fleet of staff – the cook, the maids, the butler and the footmen, who paled into insignificance when they were not serving – James and Diana had the house to themselves. At Highgrove the detectives slipped into the background. Diana and James were hardly aware of them.

What they both enjoyed more than anything else about those weekends was the apparent normality of them, that at last they were able to feel like any other couple who were so pleased to be together that it did not matter what they did. They just wanted to be, to soak up each other's company, to feel the reassuring hand and the electrifying glow of each other's presence.

Diana would sit watching James read, noting the way he carefully folded back the pages of the newspaper so as not to overcrease them, too aware of her happiness to concentrate on reading anything herself. She wanted to go inside herself, to reflect, to savour this feeling. Then her excitement would make her restless, and she would chivvy James along and together they would go to the stables and watch the boys mount and ride around the adjoining field. As James leaned against the fence,

Diana by his side, issuing encouragement and gentle advice, Diana felt that she was experiencing a taste of all she had ever wanted.

For her ambitions had not been to walk a red-carpeted globe, not to inspire universal adoration, but to create the one thing her childhood had denied her. She had lain in her bed at Park House and at Althorp dreaming of the happy family unit that she would surely build. She would envisage the loving husband who would stand so firm and proud at her side. She would see his unparalleled joy when she presented him with a child, how he would look at her with an intensity that said she was the cleverest woman alive.

She felt a twinge of sorrow when she remembered how, when she had first shown Charles their new baby Harry, his tone had been almost dismissive as he had merely commented that it was a boy and that he had rusty hair and soon afterwards had left her for the polo field. It was at that moment that she had felt that a part of her had died, a part of her that, however badly she wanted him to do so, her husband could not rekindle. He had hurt her so terribly that, in order to survive the crushing blow, she had closed a door that she knew she could never reopen. She realised then that it was the beginning of the end of her marriage.

Now, as she watched James so proficient with her sons, she allowed herself the indulgence of thinking what a good father he would be, how kind yet disciplined; how keen he would be for his children to do well but how, even more, he would want them to be happy. If only, she thought, she could marry this man, if only she could give him a child; for here was a man who would stay by her, a man who, once he had pledged his word, would never forsake her for another.

During those weekends they would sit for hours in the calm of the early evenings by the thyme walk of Charles's herb garden, drinking the perfume so rich after a day of warm sunshine. They would walk slowly round the gardens, arm in arm, through the rose walk overhung with musky-scented blooms. All the treasures of this garden, the manicured lawns, the subtle shades of colour in the herbaceous borders, the fat roses spilling over bushes, the carefully-tended pathways, the honeysuckle sweeping from central staves with its tentacles trailing the ground, all these added to James and Diana's pleasure, their sense of freedom and perfection.

However, it was the sheer perfection that unsettled James deep inside. Because he had never felt so fulfilled before, he feared that unless he was with Diana and this love was kept alive he would never feel like this again; that having reached the summit, he would always ache with the strain of keeping his muscles taut for the solitary descent. A brooding melancholy would sometimes dim his vision and it was almost as if he was gearing himself up for the lonely exile of life without her.

Diana, sitting snugly by his side, was locked in her ecstatic world of reverie. In her ideal existence, all she would need all her life would be to be loved and needed by this man. She wanted to hold on to her dream, to indoctrinate herself with the belief that, if she truly wanted it badly enough and prayed for it wholeheartedly, it would become a reality.

Diana was so sensitive that she could always detect a companion's slightest emotional flicker. She knew in an instant when James was beginning to close down, the second that he was pulling back. She always felt that there was a part of him that she could not reach. Then she would feel the first swell of panic, the old fears that she was losing him. She would entreat him over and over to share with her his private worries, his deepest thoughts. Pleading, she tried to make him see sense, to see that, because she loved him so much, she could feel his deep inner loneliness as if it were her own; that just as he helped her, she desperately wanted to help him. Unless he was really honest, unless he allowed his vulnerability to show, there would always be a distance between them and that was unbearable to her.

It was to little avail, for the last thing that James wanted to do was to burden the fragile Diana with his own misgivings. He felt that it was his duty to keep her as free from anxiety as possible. So he would close the door on his feelings and clothe himself in the impenetrable armour of falsehood. And in convincing Diana that he was fine, that he was deliriously happy, that of course they would always be together, he would briefly convince himself.

In the evenings, after they had bathed and changed, they would return to each other. Those too were relaxed, happy times. They would watch television, flick through magazines and play James's favourite game of choosing a house for them to live in from the pages of *Country Life*. After a few drinks, James would feel his previous melancholy slip away and his total absorption in Diana return.

He greatly enjoyed eating at Highgrove as the quality of the food was very high. Diana would choose the menus which the cook would execute to perfection. The food was always fresh and seasonal. In summer they ate poached wild salmon, asparagus, fat garden peas and buttery new potatoes followed by summer pudding and thick, clotted cream; in winter they were served local game followed by pies and puddings with jugs of steaming custard. As usual James ate with relish and was delighted to notice that he could mark the happiest times as those when Diana ate more. Of course there were months when she was distressingly thin and would barely eat, but he thought it best never to pass comment.

The summer days were the finest, centred around the swimming pool. Diana had always loved swimming, had always felt soothed near expanses of water. In fact swimming had become something of an obsession for her. Whenever she felt overemotional, she would pound up and down the pool, thrashing the tension out of her body with every length. She felt supported in the water and strangely immune. Whatever was going on in her head, whatever anxieties were trying to take over, she knew she could override them as now it was she who had control. She felt the power of her body once again as she cleaved so elegantly through the water. Afterwards, as she sat on the poolside, her heart beating, her face flushed, she felt calmed and cleansed.

The first thing that her father had done when he took on the title Earl Spencer and moved his family from Norfolk to Althorp, the seventeenth-century family seat in Northamptonshire, was to build a swimming pool. Diana told James that most of her happiest memories were of larking around by the pool with friends and shooting down the slide into the water. The pool at Highgrove was heated all year round, and whenever she relapsed into her obsession with her figure, she found that she needed to swim more and more. She used to rise at dawn and in winter cross the snowy ground to the pool, and she would often also swim late at night – on one occasion tripping over a ladder in the dark. More recently, however, she had realised that there was a fine line between fitness and madness; that a healthy body, while beautifully toned, was a yielding one, not a thin stick beaten daily into submission.

James loved playing with Diana and the boys in the water. Boisterously, they would horse around, throwing balls, racing and lightly ducking one another. He would wrap Diana in a towelling robe as she came out of the water, and they would often have long lazy teas by the pool or else more formal, but equally relaxed, lunches served with perfectly chilled white wine.

The only other visitors who shared their cosy weekends were Carolyn and William Bartholomew. Carolyn, a friend of Diana's from West Heath school, was Diana's oldest and most trusted friend. As she had shared a flat with Diana after leaving West Heath, she had witnessed at first hand her formal courtship with Prince Charles and, a few years later, was as devastated as Diana to discover that the marriage was not working out.

A true, caring friend, she told Diana not what she wanted to hear but what she needed to know. A balanced woman, with no axes of her own to grind, secure within herself and generous-spirited, she loved Diana enough always to speak plainly. When Diana confided in her about her bulimia, years into the illness, Carolyn urged her to seek help and would not let the matter rest until she had found Dr Lipsedge and started treatment with him.

So happy in her own marriage, to brewery heir and party-planner William Bartholomew, Carolyn could not help but want Diana somehow to find the same happiness. Theirs was a rare friendship, based not on one-upmanship and petty rivalries but on true affection.

Both Carolyn and William were greatly saddened when they discovered the extent of Diana's unhappiness, especially as they had always liked and got on with Prince Charles. More than anything, though, they longed to see Diana back to her old cheerful self. Carolyn could not bear to see this pale, wan creature who would come to visit her in her Fulham home and often sob as she poured out her troubles.

So she could not have been more delighted when she saw the cheeky sense of fun rekindled in Diana. Both she and William thoroughly approved of James. They had no wish to condone adultery, far from it. Yet they knew from Diana about her husband's affection for Camilla Parker-Bowles and they had feared for Diana's emotional welfare.

Being with Diana when she was with James was like being with the Diana of old, the sunny girl they feared they had lost for ever. They both liked and got on with James in a wholesome, chummy manner. They watched with the relief of anxious parents as they saw how good he was for Diana, how he had restored her self-esteem, how, in his quiet, attentive way, he comforted and strengthened her. And in their private, giggly moments, Diana would confide in Carolyn and tell her intimate details, how much James excited her.

They were an extremely jolly and noisy foursome, filling the house with shrieks of laughter and good, innocent fun. There were no airs and graces, no pretensions, merely four friends enjoying one another's companionship and the simple country pursuits. They would take long walks followed by hearty teas, play rowdy games of tennis, giggle and gossip late into the night or watch videos until the early hours. They all shared a love of music – Carolyn had recently completed a course in opera at the Royal College of Music – and they would all enjoy listening to a rousing opera or concerto.

Diana was thrilled that they brought Highgrove alive for her again and allowed her to enjoy being there as never before – for she had come to hate the house as she knew that it was the place where Charles and Camilla felt most relaxed, where *they* spent *their* happiest times. She knew the sour fact that in her absence Camilla was mistress of her house, that the staff of Diana's domain were unwittingly involved in the whole charade. So for Diana the house had come to have nothing but wretched associations with Camilla. Everywhere she looked, she would imagine Camilla's touch. She knew her husband's routine and, fraught with despair, she envisaged Camilla being a part of it.

And then, when she wanted to rouse the dormant demons in her mind, when she wanted them to convince her how worthless she really was, she would focus on her jealousy. Her hatred for Camilla was frightening in its intensity, a dynamic, suffocating loathing of this woman whom she held to be the root of all her problems. She taunted herself with the miserable thought that this woman had denied her what she wanted most from life, had stolen what was hers by right. For in her own eyes Diana had had everything in the world except the one thing that meant anything to her – the love of her husband.

That was for Camilla. She would imagine Camilla and Charles together and she would know that when Camilla entered Charles's study she was genuinely welcomed, that unlike her, Camilla would not be met with a bored stare but with a loving look of surprise and delight.

If James was with her she could just about control her rage when she returned to Highgrove and found that little things had been changed, that the flowers had been arranged in a particular way and that the staff had been ordered to serve things in a different manner. But if she was alone, waiting for Charles and the boys to arrive, she would be filled with fury that this woman had the power – worse, was given the power by *her* husband – to run *her* house as she thought best. She had the power to entertain his guests – their guests – to tell the butler when to clear, to take the ladies after dinner and make sure that they were comfortable, to see if they needed anything – to see if they needed anything from *her* house, possibly from *her* bathroom. Then, teetering on the edge of hysteria, she would ring James.

James would do his best to soothe her, to tell her that he

understood how difficult it was for her. He would remind her
to try to be strong and not to let Charles see how badly the
situation got to her. He told her that if she could find her own
strength, the situation would lose its grisly hold over her, and
that jealousy was such a negative, destructive emotion that
it was a waste of time to give it any energy. He knew this
because it was an emotion that he, for the first time, was
himself endeavouring to learn how to deal with.

James did not approve of jealousy, had long ago convinced
himself that it was a shameful feeling, that a man should always
have sufficient confidence to override the petty insecurities that
were the root of this evil. But now, increasingly, he was coming
face to face with this irrational emotion and he did not know
what to do with it.

Thinking about it reminded him of when he had watched on
television the breathtaking sight of Diana dancing with Prince
Charles during their recent official visit to Australia. Wearing
an off-the-shoulder cream chiffon dress patterned with blue
flowers and a sapphire and diamond necklace as a headband,
she had been positively electric, outstandingly dazzling and
alive. As he watched Prince Charles swirl his radiant wife
around the floor, James had felt leaden with disappointment,
let down, betrayed.

He had given so much to Diana, he had been prepared to
give her his last breath so that she might be resuscitated and
live fully again, and yet here she was dancing so intimately with
a man she had said did not love her – a man who she had said
had broken her heart, whom therefore, she said, she now hated
with a vitriolic intensity.

Of course, it was not in James's nature to express anger, so
when Diana rang him as usual the next day, he simply asked
about her trip and he did not mention in any great detail the
dancing scene that the press was so full of. Diana, immediately
sensitive to his quiet reserve, aware that he was holding back,
asked him what was wrong. Eventually she squeezed his dismay
out of him: it pained him that, when he had thought that she
loved him, all he had been able to see on that dance-floor was
her look of love for her husband.

As she reiterated her love for James, she begged him to
see the truth. Of course she loved him, she said, more than
she had ever thought possible. He knew better than anyone
what was really going on, that her marriage to Charles was
a sham, steeped in falsehood. He must know that these trips
were difficult, that it was her job, her duty, to appear radiant
and happy, that Charles expected her to keep up the façade
in public – but that the minute the camera shutters were
closed, once the official handshakes were over, he retreated
from her. She told James that then she felt so far from home,
and so far from him, that she lay alone at night imagining him
by her side, and counted the days until she would be with
him again.

James felt sure that Prince Charles must know about his love
for Diana, but if he did, he never let on. They would see each
other at polo matches from time to time and, as always, Prince
Charles would be friendly and polite.

On one occasion, after a match at Smith's Lawn, James
was unwinding in the Dunhill tent, chatting, glass in hand,
to a young female polo groupie, when Diana, perhaps feeling
slightly threatened, arrived at his side to say hello – she was
always charming to James in public, expressing as much
delight at seeing him as she could possibly get away with.
Suddenly James noticed Prince Charles crossing the marquee
towards them. He felt a flash of panic wash over him, yet his
demeanour was as unflinchingly calm as usual. He had no
idea what Prince Charles was going to say, how Diana was
going to react or how he himself was going to feel. To his
relief the Prince was nothing but friendly and merely asked
how the riding lessons were going. James said that they were
going very well, thank you Sir, and that Her Royal Highness
showed signs of great promise, to which the Prince replied that
he was very pleased.

To see Diana standing there with her husband, giggling
as James praised her riding, filled James with a strange
disquiet. He noted the slight hint of reserve with which they
communicated but it did not help. He could not deny that again

he was feeling jealous. However real his and Diana's love was for each other, when Diana stood at Charles's side she was a wife standing by her husband, and that was a bond that James could not break, even if he had wanted to. But having to face the seemingly impenetrable links of that union reaffirmed his own delicate position, fuelling his feelings of helplessness. Why was it that they could only ever be together in private, could only sneak off to express their love, had to shroud their feelings in secrecy? Of course, on one level, he knew very well why, but sometimes it filled him with a frustration that was hard to bear.

Lately he had felt the urge to break free from his measured control and share his passion with the world. Why did he have to stand here so correct and ambivalent when all he wanted to do was climb the highest steeple and scream the truth to the heavens until he had no voice left?

Saying goodbye to the Prince and Diana, and watching them walk away together, he reflected that Prince Charles was perhaps grateful to him for making Diana happier. Charles was surely content for her to do her own thing as long as the status quo was not ruffled. After all, Charles had evidently always presumed that in that area they would lead separate lives anyway, and had never seemed able to understand why she had taken so long to grasp this, why she seemed unable to accept it.

On the whole James was proud that he appeared to be keeping Diana from going under. She kept telling him how much better she was feeling, how happy he made her and how she saw him as a sort of prize for all her previous suffering. He could see the look of fear fade from her eyes as they spent happy weekends together at Highgrove, and he was glad. Yet he still met with great displays of instability which shocked and frightened him. Often on Sundays, as the afternoon drew on and James was already mentally preparing for his week ahead, Diana would begin to falter. She knew that he would have to leave soon, to drive back to the barracks, and often she would lose her self-control. Suddenly all she could focus on was her own week ahead, her lonely nights at Kensington Palace, and

she would feel desperate – as desperate and low as a child who
has to return unwillingly to boarding school, to leave a safe
nurturing place and face the unpredictability of others and the
pressures to conform.

She would dread his departure and afterwards hate herself
for making it so difficult for him. Yet every departure, although
she knew it was necessary, struck her as a form of rejection.
That he had no choice but to leave did not help the fact that
she would be left alone and afraid, did not prevent her from
feeling as she watched his car turn the corner of the drive
that her strength and courage were going with it. The next
few days would seem interminable. She could not cope with
the sinking feeling, the sack of trauma she feared she could
never lift.

As James was preparing to leave, she would go to him and
as he took her in his arms she would often cry a child's tears
of fear of abandonment. She would cling tightly to him, and
he would hold her reassuringly, trying to infuse her with all
the strength he had. Often Diana would need confirmation
of his feelings, would need a last taste of passion to hold on
to, to cherish. On one occasion she was fiddling about in her
bathroom and James went in to say goodbye; he said that he
really must go, and he thanked her for an unutterably lovely
weekend. Diana fell into his arms and after she had kissed him
she said that she needed him; needed him now; wanted him
there and then.

At times her need scared him. After long discussions on
the telephone when she had poured out her heart to him, he
would feel that because he was not physically beside her he was
powerless to help and he was afraid, afraid of what she might do.
He never failed to be astounded by the emotional rollercoaster
she lived on. Just as he had relaxed in the conviction that she
seemed so much more balanced and happy, just after she had
assured him that really she was not letting things get to her
so much, her resolve would crack and violent paroxysms of
despair would take over.

The intensity of these outbursts shocked him, but he did
not know how to save her. He knew how much of his love

and energy she needed, but he did not know if he was able
to provide it. Then he felt gripped by desperation himself, and
fretted that he could not possibly convince her how special she
was and how much strength she had in her, if she would only
trust herself and find it.

During this time Diana was becoming increasingly involved
with the charity work of her choice. Over the years she had
built up a diverse portfolio of presidencies and patronages,
but it was her work with AIDS sufferers that gave her
particular satisfaction. She took all her charity work extremely
seriously, not just because she was genuinely interested in the
charities to which she pledged her name but also because she
needed constant confirmation of her own worth. She wanted
reassurance that she did have an important role to play, a
role that she would prove to her husband and his family
she was eminently capable of executing. They would not be
able to dismiss her as fickle, as half-hearted in her attempts
to spread some good, if, for example, as patron of the British
Deaf Association she took the trouble – as she did – to learn
sign language.

As she stepped outside her safe circle of childhood friends
and her interests widened, she found that she was striking up
new and enduring friendships such as that with Adrian Ward-
Jackson, the deputy chairman of the AIDS Crisis Trust.

Adrian was to have a tremendous influence on Diana. A
profoundly spiritual man who had known since the mid-1980s
that he was HIV positive, he had a tremendous faith and belief
in life. What he made her see was that perhaps there was reason
in her own deep unhappiness; that if she had never suffered, she
would never have grown; that if she had remained the naïve,
cosseted girl of her childhood locked in her world of dreams,
she would not have been able to reach others with the sincerity
that showed she really cared; that perhaps she had needed to
have the shock and the betrayal to force her out into the harsh
light of the real world.

She had to see clearly, to face the bitter truth of life, or she
would never have been able to help people. For it is only

when you yourself have sunk to your knees in despair that you recognise and understand when others are similarly crippled, and then instinctively your heart reaches out to them. If you have never stood on a cliff edge, you do not know what it is like to want to jump.

Diana found that visiting the homeless, the sick and the dying gave her a sense of purpose. It reassured her to know that she could justify her past unhappiness because here she was intuitively feeling other people's pain. Just as she was desperate for love and affection, to be touched, to be made to feel special, so she knew that they must be. These experiences helped to bring her back to reality: they were a sober reminder that, behind the smart clothes, the jewels and the grand titles, she was just flesh and blood like the rest. Her needs were their needs and vice versa.

She was genuinely interested in listening to others, in comforting them with her undivided attention, because she not only experienced pleasure in being able to relate to them and relief in knowing that she was not alone with her feelings, but also found that in homing in on someone else's pain she temporarily forgot her own.

7

Just as Diana was eager to share every aspect of her life with James, so James wanted Diana to know every facet of his existence. As their affair progressed, past the summer of 1987 – when the press made a grand fuss because Diana and Charles were apart for thirty-nine days – and on into the early months of 1988, James was conscious that Diana had not met his mother. He was not happy with the fact that she had met his father while his mother was unaware of full extent of their relationship. It did not seem right.

Also, having enjoyed so many weekends of undiluted comfort at Highgrove and merry, pampering dinners at Kensington Palace, James was keen to return a measure of Diana's generous hospitality. He wanted her to come and stay at his home in Devon, to cosset her on *his* territory.

Shirely Hewitt was used to James bringing girlfriends home. She prided herself on the fact that he felt comfortable inviting them for the weekend as he knew that no awkward questions would be asked, that they would largely be left alone. He knew that she considered and treated him as a grown man and would never have dreamed of meeting any of his behaviour with disapproval.

So when James casually asked his mother if he could bring a friend home for the weekend, she said that of course he could, gently enquiring if it was anybody she knew. James told her simply that it was the Princess of Wales and without batting an eyelid Mrs Hewitt merely asked what bedroom she should put her in. James said his bedroom. And that was that; it was dealt with cleanly. Now she knew. In that marvellous stoical manner that only the British can muster, there had been no drama, no unseemly, prying questions. Shirley Hewitt had dealt with it as she dealt with everything, with tremendous aplomb. Her lip had not so much as quivered.

The first time Diana came, she drove down with her detective Ken Wharfe, her green Jaguar followed by a back-up car containing four policemen. They stayed round the corner in a local hotel, while Ken Wharfe slept in the Hewitts' spare bedroom. James thought that the four police were perhaps unnecessary and feared that they would draw too much attention in this quiet Devon village, but then he reflected that since her marriage Diana had never been away anywhere without this level of protection.

She arrived early on Friday evening and James, feeling mildly apprehensive, was waiting for her in his study which looks out on to the road. As soon as he saw her car, he opened the study stable door which doubles as a front door and went out to greet her.

Diana was thrilled to see him, to be at his home. She had enjoyed the drive greatly, she told James, who knew that behind the wheel she gained a sense of freedom, of being in control. She did not tell him then that she had spent the last leg of the journey wondering what the house was like, what his mother would be like and whether they would get on. Having relished meeting his father and sisters, she had had few doubts, but you never knew with mothers and sons; they could be tricky, not to mention possessive. It reminded her of the way that the Queen could undermine her with a simple look of searching incredulity as if Diana were an alien, an alien whom, moreover, the longer she studied, the less able she was to understand what all the fuss was about.

Diana knew that James loved his mother dearly – he had spoken of her often, his eyes full of respect – and she knew that it was important that his mother like her and that she in no way disapprove of the situation. She knew from James that Mrs Hewitt too had been deeply wounded by her own marriage breakdown, and hoped that that common link would fuel a certain empathy and even friendship.

Diana need not have worried. The moment James led her

through his study, with its low ceilings striped with dark oak beams, and into the sitting room where his mother was waiting, she knew that she was going to be all right. As she looked at Shirley Hewitt's kind face, her soft body and the lines of understanding on her forehead, she instantly felt that here was a friend, a woman who had suffered in her own quiet way, who would not judge her or expect anything of her. She could have guessed and felt reassured that while in her own wise way Shirley Hewitt missed little in life, she did not think that it was her place to comment.

Diana smiled at James's mother, relieved that she was the antithesis of so many she had come across in royal circles. Thank goodness James's mother was not tarnished with any hint of a haughty gaze or shadow of an intimidatingly severe posture. Rather it was as if a silent understanding, a flicker of recognition, were passing between them.

As she looked round the room, Diana felt comfortable, for the Hewitt household was not ostentatious. Unlike so many houses she visited, it was not cold and grand or ridiculously pretentious with endless swags of expensive chintz. Rather it was the simple, functional home of a military family, with that slight air that diplomatic homes often have of people passing through.

She loved the fact that this old, low house, tucked snugly into a bend in the road, was not threatening, that it did not have cavernous rooms which merely exacerbated your loneliness. Instead, its low ceilings enveloped you with protective concern. The walls were close enough together to see what was going on.

As with many good old-fashioned sporty families, it was easy to see where the Hewitts' priorities lay. Not just in James's quarters, which were a shrine to his bachelor sporting existence, but all over the house was evidence of horses and dogs. Although the house was much smaller, the atmosphere reminded Diana of her early childhood home, Park House, with its somehow dated feel. It was as if she was in a time warp, and she found it reassuring.

James could not get over how odd it felt to watch his mother curtsy to a woman with whom he was so intimate, but he felt proud of them both as they put each other at ease. While Mrs Hewitt showed Ken Wharfe to his room, James led Diana up the winding stairs from his study to his bedroom. As she stood at the top of the stairs, looking at James's two walnut-backed single beds, she wanted time; time to survey this room which spoke reams about the man she was so in love with. And she loved him all the more for the schoolboy still in him. She felt a burst of tenderness as she looked at the walls covered in team photos, at the mementoes of his action-man heroics. This was a purely masculine domain, a room that he had made his private world, which showed no concessions to the women in his life, and she felt strangely honoured to be a part of it.

Downstairs Mrs Hewitt was pouring tea and, as they descended, both James and Diana were struck by the utter naturalness of the scene. As Diana sat in the comfortable armchair closest to the fire, she felt safer than she had for a long time. This was proper family life; Mrs Hewitt, warm and friendly, presided over the teapot, carefully making sure that no one went without. It was this cosy level of attention and domesticity that Diana had long been seeking, where there were no conditions, where she did not have to perform to gain approval, where she could feel confident that she was loved.

Shirely Hewitt may not have had her husband by her side but there was still very much a sense of familial solidarity in the house. You had only to listen to the easy communication between mother and son to know that beneath the surface respect was an implicit love that did not need to be articulated, a stronger, purer love perhaps as it did not demand constant confirmation.

Diana and James left Ken Wharfe chatting with Mrs Hewitt and slipped away upstairs to be alone. Diana needed to be in James's arms, needed him to dispel the traces of the state of emptiness she fell into when he was not with her. While she reassured herself that she was working hard to solve her own difficulties, she still needed James's warmth to comfort her and soothe her ragged nerves.

There were to be many more weekends like this in Devon. Often while Diana was bathing in James's well-appointed bathroom, with its elegant mahogany table on which lay his grooming implements and a pile of old hardbacks of romantic poetry, James would take Ken Wharfe to the local pub for a few pints. He might leave a page of Shakespeare's sonnets or some florid Tennyson or Wordsworth open and prominent. As Diana lay there and soaked this in, she would be moved and touched by the message he wanted to convey. She loved it when he read to her, his low, smooth voice carefully enhancing the words. He often used passages from his favourite poetry as a means of expression, as he found it difficult to speak the language of his own heart; it was easier to distance yourself by reading out somebody else's more eloquent declarations of passion. Although he denied being a romantic, would make light of it with a mock chauvinistic remark if she tried to force him into some sort of admission, Diana was entranced by his hidden romantic sensitivity.

James liked Ken Wharfe immensely and was glad that his liking was reciprocated. For Ken grew fond of James and thought very highly of him. Furthermore, he seemed to like what James did for Diana, approved wholeheartedly of the way James calmed her, how happy he made her and how different she was in his presence. To a certain extent, James took the pressure off Ken. This kind, loyal detective had borne the brunt of a great deal of Diana's unhappiness and since James had come on the scene, Ken had been able to step back.

Ken was a pleasure to be with; he had achieved the perfect balance between caring confidant and official bodyguard. While friendly, he was never overfamiliar, and with his penchant for a good laugh he fitted into the Hewitt household with ease.

Evenings were always the merriest times, flooded with peals of laughter. Diana did not think that she had ever seen James this relaxed. She loved watching him play the role of host, loved his attentiveness. They would follow Mrs Hewitt into the dining room as if they were one family, easy and without standing on ceremony. In the low, cosy dining room, around the long polished table covered with the regulation silver – the tall candlesticks and the silver pheasants trailing their feathers down the centre panel – a tacit understanding and kinship would hold sway.

If James's sisters came to dine, they would unite with Diana, and James would be the focus of much loving teasing. If he was standing at the sideboard carving the game, he would hear only their silvery giggles and feel flattered that their hilarity more often than not sprang up good-naturedly at his expense. Because Diana loved him so, all she really wanted to talk about was him. She adored hearing stories about his childhood, would ask Mrs Hewitt endless questions, and threw back her head with squeals of delight when James's seriousness or his sartorial perfectionism was gently mocked.

Often they would crowd round the fire until the early hours, the women gossiping and sipping away at some sweet, exotic liqueur while James and Ken nursed a few whiskies. Eventually James and Diana would return upstairs to their haven. They would push his two single beds together and relax in the knowledge that in this house they could enjoy the hours of night like any other loving couple.

When they were together, they wanted no attachment or responsibility beyond the moment. Those weekends were like an eternity trapped in a few hours. Only the present took on any significance; the future was too distant to matter, too uncertain to contemplate. They had to take care that Diana was not recognised, so they rarely left the house. That they never felt the itchy discomfort of claustrophobia was testimony to the strength of their union.

James unlocked latent desires of new-found intensity in Diana and, as they had so few full nights together, they spent a good proportion of those weekends languishing in each other's arms. They longed for Sunday mornings, those long playful hours when they lay peacefully together, the sheets threaded through the tangle of their bodies. The stress of their secret meant that when they could be together as freely and as naturally as this, they started to let go, allowing themselves to become tired and sleepy. Those weekends, those hours of semi-sleep and deep relaxation, revived and replenished them.

That they did not feel so much as a twinge of embarrassment as they descended for breakfast, which was by now lunch, on Sunday mornings says much for Mrs Hewitt's sang-froid. Yet it was because they were so deeply in love that what might seem curious to everybody else seemed completely natural to them. Blinding love was just that: blinding. Everything slipped smoothly by without effort. There was no room for gauche, prickly emotions.

Mrs Hewitt loved Diana, seeing her as special, a fragile beauty who deserved the devotion that her son was so willing, so glad to give her. She felt proud to witness, even to be a part of, such purity of feeling, and it touched her deeply.

In March 1988 Diana had to join Prince Charles and his party for his annual skiing holiday in Klosters. As usual she felt alienated and unhappy among his family and friends. Prince Andrew was there with a pregnant Sarah; Charles's friends the Palmer-Tomkinsons and Major Hugh Lindsay were also among the party. Major Lindsay, a former equerry to the Queen, had not brought his wife Sarah, a friend of Diana's who worked in the Buckingham Palace press office, because she was pregnant and preferred to remain at home.

Diana spent most of the time holed up in the chalet feeling sick and miserable. Her bulimia was back and she had a streaming cold. Yet the deep sense of foreboding that gripped her as she sat by the fire or lay on her bed seemed worse than her usual melancholy. She was aware that she felt particularly, strangely vulnerable, as if her intuition was preparing her for a new trauma. She telephoned James constantly. She could not cope with her sense of loss; she needed him now more than ever, she said.

And then it happened. Prince Charles's press secretary,

Philip Mackie, broke the news that there had been an avalanche and that one of the party was dead. When they discovered that it was Major Lindsay, Diana did not stop to consider her feelings, to pander to her own grief. Swiftly and efficiently, on an emotionally blank automatic pilot, she set about dealing with the practicalities. Where it came from she did not know, but suddenly she had the strength to cope with the situation, the initiative to take control. Like a mother who can lift a car to free her trapped child, Diana created the momentum that swept them all along. They must return with the body. They must go to Hugh's wife, she said. Those were the priorities.

Stunned from the shock and numbed with distress, Prince Charles did not at first see the importance of returning immediately to England. His friend Patti Palmer-Tomkinson had badly injured her leg and had to undergo a lengthy operation. Perhaps they should stay in Switzerland to sort things out.

Diana was adamant. They must go and be with Sarah Lindsay. Her heart was already with Sarah, and she knew that she must do everything in her power to help her grief-stricken friend.

Afterwards, when she had had time to get over the shock, James visited her at Highgrove. She lay in his arms and cried and cried, allowing him to take some of her strain. Then, pushing up through her anger, she felt the first sign of self-recognition. She had to admit that she was proud that of all of them, in that moment of panic and crisis, she had been the calmest. She had acted with a maturity beyond her years. But why could Charles never credit her with this? Why did he refuse to see what she was about? She felt as if she was climbing a steep mountain weighed down by great heavy boots when she tried to approach him. She was exasperated with the effort of trying to get through to him. Now, instead, she would honour her own sensitivity, her ability to cope. At least it seemed that through all the horror she had been given a sign that finally she was starting to heal, starting to find and make use of her own strength.

After her return from Switzerland, when the claustrophobia of the Palace had got too much, she had driven to a Dorset beach. Her head bowed low, wearing the damson-coloured Puffa jacket that James had given her, she had walked the lonely shingle and once again forced herself to accept the unpalatable truth. Her marriage was over. Their time was up. It was as if on this cathartic walk she realised that if she was to begin a new life she would have to learn to lay the ghosts of her disappointment to rest, that she was going to have to begin to trust life, to let it guide her. After all, some good had come of all this: James had come into her life and helped her to find herself.

Diana longed for those Devon weekends which – paradoxically, because her movements were more restricted than ever – represented a vital burst of freedom for her. Having dispensed with the police back-up car, she would drive Ken Wharfe or Detective Sergeant Allan Peters down herself. Often by the time she arrived she was so excited, so needy for James that she would push him straight upstairs to his room so that they could be properly united.

As her green Jaguar parked outside did not appear to cause any local comment, James and Diana became slightly braver. They would wrap up and go for long romantic walks along Exmouth and Budleigh beaches, her detectives a discreet distance behind. Diana loved to be beside the sea. It was as if in the roar of the wind and the repetitive thudding of the waves she could find, for a few moments, her own silence.

James had always had a deep appreciation of nature; it gives so much, he always thought, and demands nothing but respect in return. As he shared his knowledge of it with Diana, his intimacy with everything he saw introduced her to a new world. His world. When they were driving across Dartmoor, both of them appreciative of and sensitive to its rolling beauty, James might slowly bring the car to a halt to point out a bird camouflaged in the mossy undergrowth. Silently they would sit and watch it twitch about and, in that moment of tranquillity, she would feel drawn to him in a new way.

As the weather warmed up and the high banks of the lanes broke out in rashes of yellow honeysuckle and pink dog roses, James and Diana would go for picnics in remote Dartmoor fields. James loved to be high up, surveying the moorland swelling in the sun, and it delighted him to see the glossy pink hue of Diana's cheeks after a good dose of soft Devon air.

On one occasion the atmosphere seemed particularly special. The blue sky was unblemished by cloud, and after they had eaten thick cold-meat sandwiches, tomatoes and juicy fruit, James lay back replete, content to fold Diana into him. He had persuaded her to try his homemade lemon vodka and was pleased that she had had a few sips. He, of course, had had a few glasses. His body warmed by the burning liquid, he reflected what heavenly freedom it was just to lie still with her, to kiss her lightly but no more, not to be overtaken by desire but simply to lie in quiet communion.

Diana was restless. She wanted more. For her the beauty of the moment had to be marked; she started kissing and tickling him. But James did not want any other passion now. For him the moment was perfect, already complete in itself.

Diana continued to kiss and caress him and was almost incredulous that for once she received no response. James did not want to have to spell it out, so he said nothing and just lay inert, leaving her in no doubt. Diana winced as if violated: so it was happening again; she was being rejected; he was just the same. In her irrationality, she could not see straight, and all her weary insecurities came crowding in: so it was true; she was not good enough; he had tired of her.

She felt desperate and in her despair she had to lash out. She had to wound before she herself could get wounded again. It was damage limitation, a form of protection.

'Why are you doing this?' she shouted. 'What are you trying to do to me? How could you hurt me like this?' Sullenly she half spat the last question from her lips as if she knew that it was not quite clean, not quite fair, and wanted to rid herself of it as quickly as possible.

James was tired. All night he had held her, had aroused her

when she wanted to be aroused, as he had done for the past two years. Why couldn't she see that it was because he loved her so much that he did not want to make love to her now? He was not a machine. The idea made him feel belittled, unmanly. Rather, he wanted it always to be right with her, to be special.

As he heard the mistrust in her voice and saw her fury, for the first time in their relationship he felt angry and let down. This display was unwarranted; it was ridiculous. If he had been less angry and had been able to be honest with himself, he would have seen that her rage, this capacity for emotional extremes, depressed him and aroused an acute pity. That she had been so hurt that she could behave like this, that she could suddenly and unpredictably swerve so violently off course, worried him enormously.

However, his pride was such that he was unable to comfort her. Instead he spoke in a soft, slow, firm voice. He told her that he loved her, that he always did his utmost to make her happy but that he was not a machine. He was not a button that could be pushed at will. He had needs and desires as well. Nothing was the matter. He was just tired. She must not take it so personally, so erratically.

He sat away from her and did not look at her. His face was contorted with earnest tension.

Diana could not stand this resilience. She could not believe that he could just sit back calmly and witness her in this state of distress and that he was not coming to her now, not taking her head against his chest and letting her weep out her pain. Instead he was acting as Charles had done, ignoring her in the grip of her trauma. She could not bear it any longer, and with a final scream of anger and frustration she took off through the fields.

James did not go after her. Now he was rigid with anger too. This unruly display of histrionics had stretched his patience to breaking point. It was completely unnecessary. Enough was enough.

Slowly, heavy with the strain of the previous few minutes, he packed up the picnic and strode back to the car where Allan Peters was waiting. For half an hour they waited for

Diana to return and, in that eternity, James shared some of his fears with the understanding detective. He told him that whatever he did, it did not seem to be good enough; that he feared she had been so damaged by her rejection by Prince Charles that he did not know if the scar would ever heal; that at times like this he began to think that their love was futile; that however much he tried to help Diana, it seemed his efforts turned to dust; and that he had feelings too, was not an automaton.

Allan Peters was quietly sympathetic; he said little, just that he understood. Then they sat in that wretched manly silence which many men find more dignified than detailed analysis. When Diana crept back to the car, her eyes ringed red from her tears, she slipped into the back seat and James started to drive home.

From the front seat Allan Peters scolded her for running off like that. He said that not only was it dangerous, as they had not known where she had gone, but quite frankly, to be brutally honest, it was very rude to James who had always done his best for her. Diana said nothing. Her hostility pulsated on. She would have her revenge. Nobody spoke to her like that and got away with it. Not long afterwards Sergeant Peters was transferred from his position as her private detective.

After Allan Peters's brave outburst, they drove home in silence. Diana ran straight upstairs and James, watching the stiff, self-protective movements of her body, was mortified. He felt that he had hurt her badly and that in doing so he had hurt himself. His deepest fear had been realised. The last thing that he ever wanted to do was to cause pain to any woman, especially Diana.

So sitting by her on the bed he stroked her damp cheeks and told her how very much he loved her, that he could not bear to see her in this distress, could not bear this icy distance between them. He said that all he wanted was to make her happy and that the idea that he had caused this unhappiness was devastating. Diana was curled in the foetal position, her back to him, and James lay down beside her, moulding himself around her.

He told her that she was the most beautiful woman alive, that of course he found her attractive. He had just been tired, that was all. As he held her he could feel the rigid knots of tension in her shoulders loosen, feel her yield to his touch. 'I love you, I love you,' he said softly, and Diana turned to face him. She had a childish need to hear these words, to have constant confirmation that all was well. She did not want this one part of her life which was so good and pure to be tainted. She could not bear to risk losing it, and she fell against him with deep-seated relief and gratitude. They vowed then that they would never row again, that they would share only laughter together, never tears.

James was pleased when he was invited to Prince Charles's fortieth-birthday ball at Buckingham Palace in November 1988. He knew that both the Duchess of York and Diana had been given some invitations for their friends and he was touched that Diana wanted him to be there.

It was an extremely formal, white-tie affair. The entire royal clan was present so the atmosphere was quite stiff, despite the smattering of pop stars, such as Phil Collins and Elton John, who were among the three hundred guests. All of Charles's Highgrove set were in attendance and the guest of honour was Major Hugh Lindsay's widow, Sarah. The highlight for Charles, though, was Patti Palmer-Tomkinson's entrance when she took her first tentative steps without crutches following her leg injuries.

James barely noticed the before-the-ball dinner party he was at. All he wanted to do was get to the Palace and see Diana. For him the evening would not begin until ten-thirty when he arrived. He knew that it was going to be difficult for him and Diana, that they would not be able to be alone, could not enjoy the evening as a couple, but at least he would see her. Just to be in the same room, even if it was enormous, would be enough.

At least, that was what he thought. In fact he saw very little of Diana. It was impossible to get to her. She was in the throng of Charles's family and putting up a valiant front. Nobody would have guessed from James's cheery façade that he was racked with jealousy, that every time he saw Diana throw back her head with laughter, every time she took to the dance-floor, he longed to be by her side. But his control was magnificent, and never wavered.

He talked to the Queen and the Duke of Edinburgh briefly about the regiment and riding. It was an easy conversation, as he knew exactly what to say to them, what they wanted to hear.

He moved between the tables, looking up at people's shadowy faces as he passed. He knew several of the guests from the polo field or the Life Guards so he never had any shortage of people to sit and share a drink with, or to dance with. He always felt at ease at such parties and enjoyed them. He loved the animation, the flickering faces of couples locked in conversation over the candlelit tables. Tonight, as always, he admired the flowers and the women. Never had he seen women so poised and confident, so proud of their nonchalant chic. Many of them wore their impressive jewels with the casual ease of an old scarf tossed around their smooth, pale necks. It was as if they accepted their privilege as a divine right, which it never occurred to them to question.

Diana may have been the Princess of Wales, may theoretically have been considered more influential than the lot of them, thought James, but thank goodness she had retained her freshness. Her youth and playful sense of fun may have been weighed down by pain, but they were still there, bubbling under the surface. She was definitely a breed apart, he told himself; her loveliness transcended this slightly oppressive grandeur.

At last he had Diana to himself. Although they were crowded by people, jostling and swaying on the dance-floor, at least the moment was theirs. They tried to look at each other as blankly as possible as they knew that their secret could be shattered by a suspecting glance. Fortunately nobody was really looking, but in any case they were very careful.

Full of Bollinger and a hearty breakfast, James left the party in the early hours after the band's rousing rendition of 'God

Save the Queen'. He felt slightly empty. He would not have missed this event for the world. It had been a fantastic occasion, an anachronistic scene from old England, blending the elegance of tradition with the restrained grandeur of old wealth.

However, that would not be the party whose memory he would cherish for ever. The one that he would count as one of the most special of his life came on the evening of Raine Spencer's sixtieth birthday in May 1989. Her husband, Earl Spencer, was giving a dance for her at Althorp and Diana had invited James.

James had never been to Althorp, the Northamptonshire home of generations of Spencers, but he had heard much about it from Diana and was looking forward to seeing it. What was even better, Diana had told him excitedly, was that Prince Charles was not going to attend the dance so they would have plenty of opportunity to be together.

Along with her sisters, Jane and Sarah, and her brother, Charles, Diana hosted a small table at the dinner before the dance. It would have been too obvious for James to have been invited to the dinner, which was for family and seventy close friends, so he was farmed out to one of the local house parties. James, like most of his friends, felt eminently comfortable arriving for dinner and a bed at the house of somebody he had never met, because the form was so rigid, so easy to adhere to. It rarely differed; it was just a reliable part of British tradition.

Your hostess would invariably come out to greet you after you had spent hours trying to find the discreet entrance to her drive. She would entreat one of her offspring or a guest whom she knew well to show you your bedroom and where the bathroom was, and then you were invited downstairs for a cup of tea or a drink. Conversation would be polite and informative, gentle banter and constant introductions as other guests arrived. Often you would have to share a room, possibly with someone you had already met as you might have given them a lift down from London. The arrangements were always scrupulous.

At about seven o'clock there would be much embarrassed

shuffling, as everybody was too polite to take the first bath. Eventually the house would be alive, doors opening and shutting, water running, the luxurious scent of preening filling the air.

Gradually guests would filter down to the drawing room and then the easy repartee that had greeted them would be replaced by the gilt edge of formality that dinner jackets and evening dresses force people to assume. As they stood in the imposing drawing room in polite groups, sipping champagne or spirits, the guests might have a sense of time standing still, a feeling that they were pacing themselves for the evening ahead in exactly the same way as their ancestors had done for generations.

For once the lonely façade of Althorp was lit up. The house had come alive and had lost its usual gaunt air of a derelict boys' public school. Rows of flares lined the drive, affording glimpses of the magnificent sheep-speckled parkland. Great excitement and bustle filled the Palladian entrance hall: evening wraps were taken, trays of champagne proffered and welcoming kisses tossed into the highly-charged air. James admired the cool dignity of the room: the haughty ceilings, the floor-length oils – a series of country scenes by John Wootton – the busts of various statesmen, the marble-topped tables, the Chinese urns filled with greenery and the chairs backed with the Spencer coat of arms.

Once inside the grand inner hall with its ancient gallery, James found Diana almost immediately. She had been looking out for him. She took him by the arm, kissed him briefly and then told him that she was going to give him a full guided tour of her home. She wanted him to see everything. She felt very proud of Althorp and admitted to herself that she wanted him to be impressed.

She took him first to the state dining room, where some of the guests had had dinner seated around the elongated rosewood dining table with its fifty-four matching mahogany chairs. People were milling everywhere, glasses in hand, so their tour was constantly interrupted as Diana greeted her father's guests. There was much hilarity over the electricity which had cut out for over an hour at six-thirty that evening.

All the Spencer children had invited friends so there was a mix of age-groups adding a family atmosphere to the lively formality. Eventually five hundred people were spread elegantly throughout the house. Diana and James passed people chatting on the small velvet chairs lining the family portrait gallery. More were filing through the pale yellow corridors downstairs with their cabinets of Meissen, Crown Derby, Herend and Dresden china; James could see where Diana had acquired her passion for small china ornaments.

The room he liked best was the library, the family's sitting room. With its walls lined with books, and its huge desk looking out on to the formal Italian garden, it had a happy feel. He could imagine the family taking tea around the fireplace, the children lolling on the rosy chintz sofas and red leather chairs.

Diana led him through the hall past the grand piano dotted with family photographs – James noted there was not one of Prince Charles although there were many of other members of the royal family – to the wide oak staircase, where he caught the familiar faces of politicians, local aristocracy and society figures, all smiling at Diana as they passed.

Dancing was in the long picture gallery and, as there were plenty of young people, there was rarely an inch of parquet floor not covered with jiggling feet. Diana and James danced, chatted, drank champagne and reeled with unreserved happiness. If Diana had to go and dance with someone else, James did not mind. He knew that there was no need for jealousy; this evening she was his.

James chatted to her brother Charles and his new bride Victoria, and he had a long conversation with Diana's father, Earl Spencer. He liked the Earl tremendously. He had met him a couple of times at Kensington Palace and when the Earl had visited Highgrove during their weekends, joining them for lunch or tea and staying to watch the boys ride. James could see how much Diana's father adored her, how proud he was of her and her sons. He doted on her, worrying for her when she was so thin and unhappy. He asked James now how Diana's riding was going and told him how pleased he was that she was in the saddle again. They spoke about William and Harry, what proficient riders they were becoming, and the Earl, courteous as ever, said that he was delighted that James had come to the dance.

Later, as Diana was finishing her guided tour, she took James into the small dining room upstairs where her step-grandmother Barbara Cartland was holding forth. James was briefly introduced to this legendary *grande dame* and to Diana's stepmother, Raine Spencer.

As he surveyed the grandeur of the house, the vista of interrelated sitting rooms and bedrooms, the distinguished paintings and the ornate antiques, he reflected on Diana's naturalness, on how she had been brought up among all this and yet was truly happy leaning against the Aga in his mother's narrow galley kitchen, chatting and drinking coffee. He saw that she had no real wish for the pomp and ceremony of the aristocracy; rather she longed for any form of cosy familiarity. At the same time Diana was a true aristocrat. She took people for what they were, not who they were; there was not an ounce of petty snobbery in her.

As he wandered through the house, James was struck by the profusion of splendid flowers. Majestic arrangements of white lilies and green foliage towered above the guests, who, as the champagne flowed, became louder and merrier. James drank plenty. He felt relaxed and carefree, so why not indulge?

Well after midnight, Diana took him by the hand and led him outside into the garden. They were hot and breathless from dancing, glowing all over. The night air cooled them and there was a magical quality to the ghostly light. Diana took James to the right of the house, under the gently swaying trees to the family's private garden. They walked slowly across the wet grass, smelling its freshness, and through the wall of hedges to the swimming pool. Diana opened up the french doors of the poolhouse and together they sat on an old sun-chair and looked out into the still of the night, at the sepulchral calm of the pool.

Then, softly, they spoke about their love. Between their kisses and caresses they agreed what a special evening this had been, that they had both felt so proud of each other, so pleased to be together and so at ease. James told Diana how much it meant to him to have seen her home. Now he had a greater sense of her childhood. He could picture her movements as she had walked through this great park, as she had sat by the tall windows and waited for her adult life to set her free. He scooped her into his arms and, as their kisses took on an urgency, Diana whispered in his ears. Now. Nobody will come. Nobody will find us. It was thrilling to be locked together, so near to that great throng of people and yet so intimate, so alone.

When they joined the guests filing into the Sunderland Room, their nostrils filled with the aroma of the breakfast that had been laid out. This room, with its fireplaces from Spencer House, the family's original London home, and its light rose-patterned carpet, was often used for formal entertaining. Diana laughed as James piled his plate with kedgeree, sausages and eggs. She felt so proud of him as she sat beside him at one of the small, round tables that dotted the room. They looked at each other, their eyes sparkling, and never had their secret seemed more precious, more worthwhile.

8

The acid test of Diana's resurgent confidence came when she decided to attend the fortieth-birthday party of Camilla Parker-Bowles's younger sister, Annabel. Annabel and her husband, country-house restorer and antiques dealer Simon Elliot, were a permanent part of Prince Charles's Highgrove set. As Prince Charles and Diana led almost completely separate private lives, it never occurred to him or to Camilla that the Princess would wish to appear.

However, she had a thorn in her flesh and, while she realised that she might never be able to heal the scar, she was determined to get rid of it. She discussed her intention to go to the party with James. She told him that she was no longer going to allow the Highgrove set to diminish her and that if she did not face Camilla Parker-Bowles, if she did not stare her coolly in the eye, she would never free herself from this woman's debilitating effect on her life.

James, as always, was wholly supportive. Although he disliked confrontation, as he hated to see the raw edge of people's tempers, he encouraged her. Go, he told her, and hold your head high. You have every reason to be confident. Never forget how loved and how lovely you are.

Much to everybody's surprise, a radiant Princess of Wales appeared by her husband's side at the elegant London dance hosted by Lady Annabel Goldsmith. The setting was striking, Lady Annabel's eighteenth-century mansion, Ormeley Lodge on Ham Common near Richmond, and the guests affluent and sophisticated.

Diana was fuelled by her new-found sense of self. For once she felt normal, a part of the scene. She did not feel as if she was watching from the wings, waiting until she was well enough to participate. She knew that she was as much a part of the evening as the next guest, in fact more so. This was to be her night, the evening that she had planned for years, that she had run over and over in her mind.

Now, she was too weary for revenge; she had given up hope of that. She knew that she had lost her husband and now she resented him for stealing her youth, for draining away her innocence. Now, she did not want him back; she wanted him out of her life. She knew that they would always be linked through their sons, but she no longer desired him. She hated him with a despair that had shattered her and worn her down.

It was because she no longer cared, because she did not want to walk on water for him any longer, that when the opportunity came she swept purposefully up to Camilla and told her plainly what she thought of her. Camilla was chatting in an upstairs drawing room. Calmly and with perfect control Diana took her aside and told her precisely how she felt.

Diana told Camilla that she knew that she had contributed to the failure of her marriage because she had never given up her hold on Charles, that she knew that Camilla played hostess at Highgrove in her absence and she was sickened by it, that she knew all about the breathless telephone calls, all about the endless meetings.

In those minutes, as she expressed the burning anger that had kept her rigid all those years and the frustration that had diminished her spirit, Diana reclaimed her power. She knew that the situation was irretrievable. That was not the point. She did not want her husband now. What mattered was that she had told Camilla squarely what she thought of her and what she thought of the way things were. There had been no hysteria, no undignified shouting, just the icy facts. She had spoken her own truth. Now the situation would never have the same power over her. She could begin to let go. Camilla's hold had been crushed.

Diana rang James early the next morning and recounted the events of the evening minute by minute. She told him that she felt a great weight had been lifted from her, that she felt so much freer. Suddenly the relationship between Charles and Camilla did not seem so ghastly. It was as if, by articulating her disapproval to Camilla and releasing her pent-up emotion, she had begun to accept what had happened. That did not mean that she could forgive, but she could start to put it to one side. Now she could really concentrate on her own life. All she wanted to focus on was her new-found happiness, on her life with James. Why, oh why, she wailed, had she not said all of that to Camilla sooner? What a difference it would have made.

James was to play polo in an inter-regimental final against the 13th/18th Royal Hussars, the regiment of which Diana was colonel. The match was to be at Tidworth, the place where all those years ago James had felt his first waves of tenderness for Diana when he had watched her break down in tears during her engagement. Diana said that she wanted to come and watch him, that it would be easy to do so: no one would suspect that she was coming to see James; everyone would presume that she was coming to support her regiment.

James felt buoyed up and deeply touched. He knew that actually she found polo matches quite tedious – that she had endured too many for Charles's sake – so it was definitely special that she should want to come and see him. He was proud with the thought that she would be standing there to watch him, to watch her lover.

It was to be a memorable day. James's mother and sisters were also among the spectators. Of course Diana could not be with them – she had to be in the official stand – but it was as if they all felt one another's presence and were united in their support for James.

Diana, wearing a long white flowing skirt and a black and white spotted short-sleeved top, looked translucent with happiness. She had William and Harry at her side and her gaze rarely wandered from James.

During the match James was badly hit on the arm by a polo stick. William saw a fat bruise, the size of a plum, appear and was seriously worried by it. He rushed to the edge of the field shouting James's name and would not be pacified until James had come to him and cheerfully explained that it looked worse than it felt. Then James, fulfilling his role as hero, swiftly remounted and rode back into action to finish the match.

As if to reassure him that the gods were on his side, that nothing could mar the success of the day, the Life Guards won. Diana had agreed to present the Captain and Subalterns Cup, a vast silver trophy, and James was thoroughly tickled that she would soon be presenting him with his prize. What need did he have of another? He smiled to himself. He already had the ultimate prize, the love of the most beautiful, fêted woman in the world.

Striding confidently towards her, James was aware that the effort of restraining his true feelings was pumping him with nervous excitement. As he bowed and thanked her for the cup, Diana was laughing, pretending that the cup was so heavy that she was buckling under its weight, but really she was laughing at the irony of the situation, loving every minute of their secret. Directing her eyes downward so as not to give herself away, she just caught the fleeting look that James gave her, a look that needed no explanation, that said it all.

Afterwards, when they were relaxing by the lawn, William came up to check on James, and Diana followed him over. As William started playing with Jester and the dog frolicked away, James and Diana were able to exchange a few surreptitious words out of the corners of their mouths. She said how proud she was of him, how tremendous he had looked. They both agreed how intoxicating it was to be so close, without being allowed full contact, without being able to touch. Having to pretend like this certainly heightened passion and made them hunger for their next private meeting. Diana left, and James rounded off the day with his mother and sisters in the local pub. They all seemed to sparkle; his happiness was contagious.

*   *   *

James knew deep down that the love he shared with Diana was too magical to endure. It was the stuff of fairy tales and, in terms of his life span, it would have to be ephemeral. Because their love was based on foundations of unreality, because it was their wild secret and theirs alone, it could have no real substance. It was not that their feelings were not real; quite the opposite. James had never known such searing emotion. Rather, it was his very passion that, in needing a more practical basis, would eventually define their relationship's course.

When he was alone he worried terribly. The warning bells rang louder; this could not possibly last. He had been led into a dream world, a high-octane existence of intrigue and glamour, of the most breathtaking highs imaginable and numbing, savage lows. Anything that followed in its wake would be disappointing; his life would crumble under the lead weight of mediocrity.

He loved Diana so desperately that he did not wish to curtail her joy, to dent her hope, so he concealed his worry from her. He knew that she was under intolerable pressure and he had no intention of adding to it. None the less, he knew, when he was honest with himself, that they could have no future together. Theirs was a love that could not be aired. It would not withstand the harsh light of exposure. It thrived amid the secrecy, like a damp mossy plant that flourishes close to the ground shrouded by braver foliage.

For Diana, James was her reality and that was all that mattered. Whether she really believed it or not even she did not know, but she could not bear to lose sight of her dream. So, when they were together, over and over she told him how she wanted to marry him, how she yearned to have his child.

It frightened James when she said that she would leave Prince Charles, that there had to be a separation. He did not understand her, how she could be so keen to groom Prince William for his role and be so adamant that he would make an excellent king, yet plan to distance herself formally from Charles. He tried to tell her that while British legislation might sanction divorce, the social customs of her royal world did not. Surely it was impossible.

Alone, he would feel afraid – afraid for his future. What was he going to do? He felt that he could not continue to live like this. Suddenly he wanted normality; it would be so much easier. He wanted the sort of relationship in which you could do things together, go on holiday together, spend the important times, like Christmas and New Year, together. He no longer wanted to be alone at those special times. He was beginning to feel that he needed to lay the foundations for living a proper, conventional life.

But he was trapped. How could he even contemplate leaving this woman whom he loved so much? He had never shared so much with anyone and he doubted he ever would again. He could not possibly risk hurting her. Sadly, he recognised that he was too weak to turn from her to save himself. Now he saw, for certain, that in giving her a life he was forsaking his own.

He would lie on his hard, metal bed in the barracks at Windsor feeling sad and isolated. He was too proud to confide in anyone, too locked up to go to his father now. He would stare around the bleak military room, with its small sitting room and bathroom to one side, and whenever negative feelings about his relationship with Diana entered his mind he would try to shut them off. The worst times were when he felt used. He knew that Diana loved him, but sometimes he could not eradicate the evil question lurking in the shadow of his mind: what if he was making her feel whole and reawakening her femininity for her simply to turn to another man? Whenever this notion presented itself to him he would rapidly reject it in self-disgust. That could not be; what they had was so real, he convinced himself, so special that nobody else would be able to recreate it.

It was as if Diana could hear the distant echo of his fears. She knew, at least, that he was starting to feel caged in and tried to pacify him by planning a holiday with him. They agonised over the possibility that she might be able to accompany him to the South of France where he was going to stay with his oldest and most loyal friend, Francis Showering. Francis had not met Diana, but James trusted him totally and dearly wanted to spend a week at the Showerings' beautiful villa with her. In the end, they decided that they could not risk it, so James went alone.

Once he was resting at the white, bougainvillaea-clad villa, he actually felt relieved. Not that he did not miss Diana and wish that she could have joined them, because he did. It was simply the relief of getting away from the deception. He was weary from carrying his secret. Here, he was among true friends and he could relax. He could be himself. Ever since their Millfield schooldays Francis and James had enjoyed a *Boy's Own* style of friendship; now too, in France, they carved up the chalky hills on motorcycles and spent hours dabbling about the sea in Francis's boat.

Diana could sense James's relief and it made her frantic. She yearned for him as never before and wrote to him to tell him so. If she lost him now, she would surely die. How would she have the strength to go on? She told James that every night she lay awake thanking God for bringing him into her life, that she could not believe the difference he had made to her life, could not believe the sacrifice he had made – a sacrifice that she would never be able to repay. She said that she knew he suffered for that sacrifice, suffered to stick by her, and she appreciated how much he had to cope with. Did he realise that she was aware of that suffering because when he suffered, she suffered too?

Had he any idea, she asked him, how happy he made her, and how lucky she felt to have met him? Did he have any notion of how special he was? Every minute she was apart from him, her thoughts were full of him; she lay awake at night aching with desire to be in his arms; she longed for the days when they could be together. Always. Because that was how it should be. The tears streaming down her face as she wrote, she said that she loved him more than she had thought possible. That he was her existence. Her life.

When James read the letter, he cried too.

Later in 1989, the Army was to send James to Germany on an official posting for two years. He dreaded breaking the news to Diana. One evening at Kensington Palace, after a soothing dinner, he plucked up the courage. He got just the reaction that he had anticipated. She was angry and hurt. She did not want him to go, did not want him to leave her.

Patiently James explained that while he loved her, while he could not bear the thought of a prolonged separation any more than she could, she had always known how important the Army was to him. It meant so much to him to serve his country, and he had to go. He would not be able to respect himself if he did not, and then she would not respect him either. He had to be with his men. Surely she understood more than anybody the notion of one's obligation to duty. She, who took her work so seriously, who once she had pledged her word would never renege. He had been instructed to command a squadron of tanks and he intended to fulfil the order.

Perhaps because he knew that he had to leave Diana, knew that the fault lines in their relationship were starting to appear, James began the gradual process of closing off, of shutting down because he could not bear to contemplate the pain of being without her.

And Diana, sensing his withdrawal, sensing the preparation for his flight, misconstrued it as rejection. Her greatest fear was being realised yet again: the man she loved, the man she relied upon, was deserting her, something that he had promised he would never do.

She had always been betrayed by men, she decided, and when it really came down to it she was alone. She could not bear to be this sensitive, to let every harsh word cause her such turmoil. She had to toughen up, she told herself, or she would lose the will to live.

So, in order to assuage her own hurt, in order to anaesthetise herself from further pain, she decided to block James out, to pretend to herself that she did not care that he was going away for two years. Surely if she did not see James, she told herself, she could not feel so let down, so devastated.

James did not know why she failed to answer so many of his calls. He did not understand the sudden chill in her voice when she did. The first time she was distant he picked it up instantly; it hit him like grit in the eye. The shock was savage; it sent him reeling. But still he did not know the reason. All he knew was that she was too busy to see him; her schedule was packed. She would have fought for space before, but now it seemed that she did not want to, that he was less important; he could wait.

He did. Although he knew that something serious was happening between them, he never mentioned it to Diana. If she was not going to tell him anything, he was not going to ask. It was not in him to push just then. Her sudden dismissiveness totally demoralised him; his robust self-confidence deserted him.

He would sit at his desk in his small, neat office in Windsor, staring blankly through the window at the large bare parade ground outside. The buildings and his accommodation suited his mood: they were stark and ugly. Day by day his spirit got heavier and more lethargic under the great weight of his unhappiness.

It never occurred to him to confront Diana, to ask her what was going on and why. He would simply take whatever was put before him. He would cope. He was too weak to demand her attention, too placid to make her see sense. He was too old-fashioned to allow himself the luxury of demanding an explanation and bellowing out his misery. He would never put his own feelings first. It did not seem right. He had spent so long placating women, so long pandering to their needs, that he had lost the use of his own voice.

So he kept it all in, he stuffed his emotions back down as one overrides waves of nausea. He did not have the strength to let them come up; could not cope with the force with which he knew they would hit him.

And he let Diana be. He never asked when he was going to see her, or if he was going to see her. He left the matter in her hands. When he left for Paderborn in Germany he presumed that it was over. He did not know why. All he knew was that he would mourn her and the loss of their love until he died. Only then, he suspected, would he be free.

In Germany he was glad to put his mind to his men as they afforded him regular respite from his pain. He was a professional and knew that his first responsibility lay with them. It was a tremendous relief to be obliged to shove his unhappiness aside, and to return to it only when he was alone. He thanked God for his duty, for the strength that it gave him and for the comforting sense of solidarity that he gained from being with his men.

He needed this sense of purpose more than ever now. Inside he felt helpless and grief-stricken. He knew that he must concentrate on getting through one day at a time, that the horizon was too frightening to focus on. All that mattered was that his soldiers should not sense his disquiet; it was vital that on the face of their leader they see only confidence. He threw himself into the administration of their lives as if his own life depended on it. The daily routine of looking after his men, which had once seemed rather mundane, took on a new intensity for him. It was a protective salve which kept him from himself, and he was grateful for anything that stopped him from thinking.

He was so appreciative, he reflected, as he prepared the men for tank manoeuvres, that ever since he was a boy he had been able to shut off his emotional pain; this ability which some people, principally women, considered to be his weakness he saw as a useful strength. And he endeavoured to put it to good use over Diana. He tried to accept his loss as if it were a part of him. He looked upon it as a malignant tumour: on good days it lay dormant and thankfully he could almost forget that it even existed, while on bad days he was aware of it from the moment of waking until eventually he slept.

He banished Diana from his thoughts as he taught his soldiers new skills in tank etiquette and prepared them for battle. She was allowed to flood back into his mind only at night. But then, after a hearty dinner in the mess, however hard he had tried to drown her in alcohol, she would return. How he hated those nights, hated seeing her face, feeling her soft shape in his mind, hearing her laugh and, worst of all, hearing her call out his name. His sorrow left him breathless.

Even his sport could not satisfy him. He spent his free time playing polo and hunting, but it was not enough. So, in an effort to cheer himself up, in exasperation with himself, he decided to travel. He would use his time to good effect. He did not know Germany or this part of Europe and he would learn. Surely the lure of unknown places would spark his interest?

He had already spent a lot of time alone with his misery in Paderborn, the nearest city to Sennelager where the army camp was. Standing in the hinterland where the north German plain gives way to the Teutoburger Forest, the city had an atmosphere of drama which both comforted and threatened him. He had spent many grey afternoons sitting under the dome of the cathedral, as if only this vast ancient structure had the power to help him, and he would leave feeling uplifted and reassured.

In an effort to find himself or run from himself – he was not sure which – he visited as many new cities and countries as he could. He took the train, he drove and he walked. He was always on his own; he felt too disconnected to be with anyone else.

Antwerp, Amsterdam, Munich, Salzburg, Frankfurt, Baden-Baden, Vienna, Berlin, he saw them all. He ski'd in the Alps, summered by lakes, sat for hours in cathedrals and churches and prayed that his sense of loss would lift, and that he might feel more free. He prayed that he would not have to walk the rest of his life numbed like this, fearful that however beautiful the view he would only half see it.

Occasionally Diana would telephone him, but she only made him feel worse. That they could speak this false, stiff language, that there was now so much distance between them, left him doubly sorrowful. He could not believe that they had come to this.

His last futile attempt to eradicate her essence from him, to drive the taste of her away, was to have an affair. Surely he could push her aside if he had another woman to focus on? After all, that was what he had done in the past. He had not felt attracted to anyone, not been remotely interested in any other woman for such a long time that he had begun to worry that he never would. So it came as something of a relief when he sat next to a beautiful German woman at a dance in Munich and discovered that he was quite attracted to her. Baroness Sophie von Reden was a dark, leggy, stork-like creature who intrigued James and amused him. He felt his familiar flirtatious patter return to him. It was a language that he thought he had forgotten, but once he had uttered the first rusty words it came flowing back.

James tried hard to convince himself that Sophie could wipe Diana from his mind. He wanted to believe it more than anything; it would have been so much easier. Yet he knew that he was only cheating himself, was only going to make himself feel worse.

The persistent voice of rationality told him that he should settle down, that the answer was to find a nice girl who would make a good wife and marry her. But he knew this was no use. He was further from making a commitment than he had ever been. How could he find a woman to live up to Diana? He felt sure that he would never find anyone with whom to share his life. So he picked Sophie, a divorcee with a young son. When she met James she had just parted from her husband; the timing was perfect. She needed a boost and was flattered by his attention; he needed an attractive distraction. Neither of them could even try to pretend that there was ever to be a hint of permanency.

Eighteen months after James had left for Germany, he returned to England to spend some time at home before Christmas. It was 1990 and he was keen to see his family, because war had been mooted in the Gulf, and he knew that if it broke out, he would be called upon to go.

Diana knew this too and asked him to visit her at Highgrove. And, of course, he agreed to go as he had never denied her anything, but as he drove there he was afraid. The unhappiness that had hardened around him had just started to crack and he did not want to reseal it. What if he looked at her and all the old feelings welled up but were not reciprocated? What if she spoke to him with the cool control that she had used on the telephone? He did not think he could bear that, and he wished that he had turned her down, that he had had the strength to do what *he* wanted for a change, not what she and everybody else expected of him. Why had he not said that he could not go? That he was too busy? Then, at least, he could have spared himself the potential of further hurt.

Underlying these superficial concerns, however, were violent waves of excitement. He could not believe that he was to see her again, that she had asked for him. That must mean something. Surely it indicated that all was not forgotten.

He found that his knees were slightly shaky as he got out of his car and his body was stiff with tension. He was shown into the drawing room, and the moment he saw her he knew. He had only to glimpse the excitement in her eyes to see that she was pleased to see him. There was no mistaking it, just as he could not hide his own delight at seeing her. He thought that she looked more beautiful than ever, and more mature, as if she was really coming into herself and finding the peace and strength she had worked so hard for.

They had tea and exchanged news, both fighting to keep the hint of intimacy back. They knew that they were restrained, that this polite edge jarred – but it was too soon. They were floundering in that no man's land where you are too close to speak as strangers, but have been apart for too long and are too unsure to turn to each other as lovers. There was nothing for it but to carry on, to give their conversation time to thaw.

After a while, Diana moved and positioned herself at James's feet. Too apprehensive to face him, she sat with her back to him, but she had the courage to make that crucial gesture, that sign of forgiveness. She leaned back and rested her head against his knees. Instinctively James started stroking her hair and cupping the sides of her face with his hands as they talked. It was easier this way. They could slip back together without facing each other, without looking into each other's eyes straight away.

When the tension got too much to bear, when there was no more need for these slow, sideways steps, Diana turned to James, who swept her up into his arms. Their desire seemed stronger than ever, rooted in longing and relief. Their separation had done little to dim their feelings, and their passion now was proof that it had only fuelled their need for each other.

As they lay in each other's arms, secure beneath the canopy of Diana's bed, they told each other what fools they had been. Why had they tried to deny themselves this love? It was so unnecessary. It had been so painful. Why had they tried to convince themselves that it did not exist? That it had died when it was alive and stronger than ever?

But they had no time for regrets. They wanted to savour the moment; they needed to celebrate their homecoming. As James held Diana tightly to him, he felt that every prayer that he had addressed to the heavens had been answered, that he would never forget this day. He could scarcely believe that what he had dreamed of for the last eighteen months was now actually happening; that he would not awake to face the familiar dreary disappointment. Now he was living his dream and he was alive again. If he had ever needed confirmation, now he knew. No one would ever replace Diana in his heart.

In his absence, Diana similarly had tried to block James out by developing other friendships. She needed reassurance that she was attractive, she still hungered for personal attention and, because she was feeling stronger within herself, she wanted to have some fun. She felt that she deserved it and she was determined to seek it.

All the men with whom she felt comfortable were kind and handsome. Impeccably groomed in that safe, traditional British corduroy-and-cufflinks style, they automatically sent out the right signals. They possessed the instantly recognisable code that members of the same clan pick up: the languid, arrogant walk; the right shoes; the laid-back drawl; and the nonchalance to sail through any social situation. Their manners were her manners, so she could relax with them. They were solid and non-threatening.

But however hard she may have tried, even if she may have wanted to fall in love with her escorts – such as James Gilbey and Major David Waterhouse – in an effort to purge James Hewitt from her, she found that she could not reach the same heights. She could not replace James in her affections. For what Gilbey and Waterhouse did not have was what she most wanted. Unconsciously, in James Hewitt she had found the most similar man that she could to Prince Charles, not just in mannerisms but emotionally. For when it came to women, James, like Charles, was weak.

His lure for Diana was that he was the known, so she could replay the familiar pattern of attraction – that pattern that will repeat itself endlessly unless you consciously break the chain. Physically and emotionally, James could give her everything that Prince Charles could not, and yet he felt familiar and safe. She had recognised him instantly, not realising that what she was really drawn to was a man with her husband's characteristics.

It is a cruel cycle of attraction that we lock ourselves into. Our instinctive forces tend to draw us over and over to the same situations, to the same type of people, and our observations, as children, of our parents play a large part in determining to whom we are attracted. Unless we are astute enough to see and courageous enough to shake the patterns that have been mapped out for us from birth, we are likely to repeat our parents' – and their parents' – mistakes.

As a little girl Diana perceived that all was not well between her parents, that there were needs that were left unanswered. So, without knowing it, she sought out a man who would leave her similarly empty, entered into a marriage that would be just as confusing for her children as her own parents' union had been for her.

James was also to repeat his family's patterns. He sensed as a small boy that his mother was hurting, his mother whom he loved so much, and thereafter he found himself attracted to scarred women. It was as instinctive as breathing. He was aware of Diana's need before she spoke of it, touched her deep inner pain before he touched her hand. Just as he had subtly supported his mother and gained his first sense of self-worth, the feeling that this was what it was like to be a real man, he had reached out to Diana. It never occurred to him not to be there for her. That was his role, yet it was a role that he could not declare. Just as he would deny that he loved his mother so much that it hurt, he would have to deny his love for Diana.

And for a man who was scared of commitment, who was terrified of inflicting the legacy of pain that he had seen his father bequeath to his mother, James could not have chosen better. By falling in love with the Princess of Wales, with the wife of the future King, he was ensuring that their relationship had no future. The reason that privately he could commit to her, that he could pledge his love as never before, was that he knew that that was safe, that publicly there could be no union. It was a dream that would never have to be translated into reality.

Yet the tragedy was that James had deceived himself. Thinking that Diana was safe, he allowed himself to fall in love. He did not fear the relationship, as he felt sure that he could never be trapped. So he let go and fell deeper than he could have imagined possible and, in doing so, unwittingly trapped himself. Overtaken by his love, he pledged himself to her for life. He certainly had not anticipated it. Destiny had outwitted him. He would never be free of her, never stop loving her. Emotionally he had hoisted himself with his own petard.

9

James was delighted when he heard that he was to be among those sent to fight in the Gulf War. It was an answer to his prayers. Not only was he looking forward to the challenge of putting into practice what he had learned in theory over the past sixteen years, he actually wanted to go to war as he hoped that he might die.

There would be no ignominy in death, particularly a hero's death. He had thought about it long and hard and he had decided that it would be the cleanest way.

James returned to Germany on Christmas Eve to be with his officers and his men. They were to spend Christmas Day and Boxing Day together before he flew out with a small advance party from his squadron to the Gulf.

As he lay awake on his stiff, army bed in Sennelager on Christmas Eve, feeling both happiness and sorrow, he ran over his life. Certainly it had been eventful. He had been lucky to have such a loving and supportive family. And of course, he felt that he had been chosen, that the role he had been given of loving Diana made him in some way special. Destiny, he decided, had so far steered him clear of mediocrity. But now he felt that he could no longer live with his secret torment. His last meeting with Diana had made him soaringly happy again, but he knew that it could not last. Still he could see no future. His life as he had known it was surely over.

He knew that one day their secret would be out, that they would be exposed. He feared that once the cruel forces of condemnation fixed on them, it would be over for him. The beauty of their union would surely be distorted, for how could anyone possibly understand the magic that they had shared?

He doubted that it could ever be conveyed. Then there was the danger that he might lose his army commission. The thought of leaving the regiment and his men filled him with misery. He did not think that he would be able to cope with the sense of loss.

He could not bear the thought of the infinite empty vista that would stretch ahead of him without Diana. He did not want to be relegated to an eternity of loneliness, but he saw no alternative. As much as he wanted to believe her, as much as he longed for it to be true that they could lead a life of their own together, he knew that it could not be. The wings of their hope had always been clipped.

If he could just die now in action, he thought, it would be perfect. If only he could die with their reunion fresh at the front of his mind, he would not go to his grave lonely and alone. Diana would be wretched, but at least she would be proud of him. She would not grow disillusioned with him. They would never have to discover that it could never truly last between them. They would be saved that hideous reality.

He would do anything not to have to live through another agony like that of the last eighteen months. He did not want to suffer any more; he only wanted to savour the innocent pleasure of their last, purest days.

Death seemed so dignified. Not to take your own life – he would never consider that; it would be shameful and disgracefully weak. It was the ultimate slap in the face for your loved ones, and James would never dream of embarrassing them, of besmirching their name. It simply was not an option. But to die as he had wanted to live, which was to serve, seemed glorious. There was such power in that.

He was so afraid of life, far more afraid of life than of death. Living seemed so much more difficult in comparison. It would be such a luxury to give in, to be absolved of responsibility. It was strange, he thought, as he prepared himself for his departure from Germany, that he was not remotely worried about the war, about his duties. He was so confident of his military expertise that he had no misgivings. He had a hundred and twenty men to command and twenty-five vehicles, fourteen of which were tanks, and he had supreme pride in his men. He had schooled them to think that they would go to war. He had prepared them for every eventuality and now they would be put to their biggest test. It was the challenge that he had been waiting for, the task that he knew intuitively he would enjoy fulfilling, and would do well.

No, it was not the prospect of months in the Gulf that frightened him, not the fear of action, of adrenalin pumping through you twenty-four hours a day. He was not bothered by the physical arduousness, the stress of strategy, the endless blurred days and nights when you had to keep yourself tense. These things did not frighten him, they meant that you were alive, that you were breathing and fighting for survival. You had something to fight for.

What really frightened him was his future far on the horizon, the dot that represented his life afterwards, the living death that he envisaged returning to. Unlike most of his men he had no wife or children to go back to, no life of his own. He had laid down no foundations. There was nothing that he felt was worth preserving; only the memory of Diana which death would keep alive.

He could not see himself ever marrying now. How could he ever be really pure in his heart towards another? There was no light without Diana, and he doubted that their path together would be any smoother in the future. That was why he wanted death. It would be far better to die than to live a life of merely going through the motions, of shameful repetitions for the sake of it.

James was in the perfect mental condition for war. He had been home to see his family and everything there seemed to be in order. Both his sisters were now married, living close to his mother in Devon. He had paid all his bills, written a will and, most importantly, made up with Diana. As he had set out to meet his men in Germany before heading for Kuwait, he had almost felt an inner peace. He was ready, ready to give his life for his country and for the woman he loved.

Of course he never voiced his wish for death to any of his friends or family, and particularly not to Diana. He knew that she would have been desperately hurt and would not have understood the purity of his motive.

In fact their farewell, which took place at the end of the two days he spent with her at Highgrove before leaving for Germany, had been encouraging. Inevitably there had been tears but Diana had been so strong, so selfless. It was as if she had sensed that he had regained his power, that his quest to go out and fight had rekindled his feeling of self-worth, and she had been pleased to see his old confidence; she had always been attracted to that.

She knew that this war was serious and that it meant a lot to James to go. She had nothing but admiration for his determined sense of duty. Of course she was desperate that he was leaving her again, but this time she knew that it was absolutely out of her control. Fate was leading and she could play no part except to submit gracefully. She knew that she was going to miss him more than ever because the relief of their reunion had confirmed to her how deeply she cared, how badly she wanted him to remain in her life. Yet her overriding feeling was one of pride that he was prepared to risk his life for his country – their country.

And now, for the first time where James was concerned, she had a role to play. Her husband had never really wanted the support she had been so willing to give. He had sought his solace elsewhere and left Diana feeling lacking. James too had shut her out, not in such a cold-shouldered way but by always keeping a part of himself back. Because he had always kept his needs and fears hidden from her, she had felt that he was denying her. The essence of a good working relationship, she now saw, lies in the ability of one partner to stand firm when the other is wobbling. They had never had that healthy seesaw equilibrium, where when one goes down the other automatically adds extra weight and attention to lift them.

She knew that she had been too weak before, that her well had been empty and she had had nothing extra to give, had kept every ounce of energy back for herself. But over the years, and particularly more recently, she had grown in strength. In a sense James's absence in Germany had done her good. It had made her draw on her inner reserves instead of turning to him for support; and the more she had relied upon herself, the more capable she had seen that she really was and, in turn, the stronger still she became.

Now that she had the strength to support him, she wanted to flex her power. She was glad of the opportunity to reciprocate his kindness and she determined not to fail him. It was vital that she show him how resilient she could be, reassure him that she could withstand anything while he was going through real physical danger. They might be separated but they would be together. United, they would see this thing through.

So when James was in the Gulf, every day without fail – often twice a day – she wrote to him, long, flowing letters over endless sheets of paper. She was lucid and loving, and every thought that flooded into her mind poured on to the pages. She held nothing back.

Most of all she wanted to reassure him that he was not forgotten, that he was still a part of her life. She wanted to inspire him with strength and hope, just as he had inspired her. But she also wanted to remind him of her existence. Perhaps her fear of his death propelled her; perhaps because she loved him and she knew him, she knew that he was afraid of his future life and wanted to die. How could she possibly let that happen when she felt that they had a future together? He could not leave her for ever when she could now see the faint hope that there might be a separation from Charles. Finally to have the opportunity and then only to lose him would be unbearable. It could not be. So she wrote to remind him of her love, of their love, to remind him how strong it was and how much it meant to her, how it was keeping them both alive.

Every detail of her life was saved to be shared with James. With this constant writing, with the dissection of all that was going on in her life, she felt that she was keeping James involved, ensuring that he was still a part of her. It was only when she was writing to him, when she could picture him reading her letters, that she felt a part of him. Then for a short while the dull ache of their separation was eased, and her huge sense of loss lifted a little.

*   *   *

Diana still suffered, but she was facing it. The more she examined herself and what had happened to her, the more the despair surfaced. She wanted it all out now, wanted to be free and was prepared to weather the associated discomfort. In a strange way she felt that it was fitting that she should be suffering. It was not that she felt that that was her lot, far from it. Rather, she felt that it was appropriate to be suffering with, and for, the country. Because she loved James so and felt so frightened for him, she knew that every other army wife or girlfriend was feeling the same. She identified with them more than they would know, and she wanted to help. It was almost as if God had put her in this position so that she could be of service.

She genuinely wanted to help with the Gulf War in any way she could and she fought hard to do so. Her obsession with James meant that she was obsessed with the war. Known as 'the KP war correspondent', she amazed everybody at Kensington Palace with her knowledge of strategy, tanks, sand missiles and military technique. She watched and listened to endless news bulletins, often staying up all night in the hope of hearing something about the Life Guards or, more importantly, catching a glimpse of James on television.

When John Major went out to the Gulf to visit the troops, he saw the Life Guards and the cameras caught a brief profile of James. Diana asked for a video to be sent to her, and when she had watched it and heard John Major's speech, she wrote to tell the Prime Minister how moved she had been. She told James in a letter of John Major's reply, and James thought how sweet it was and how endearingly naïve that she, the Princess of Wales, should be genuinely thrilled to get a hand-written note from the Prime Minister.

Why, she asked James, was he wearing a beret on the news clip when everyone else was wearing a hard hat? Was it, she joked, because he thought that a beret looked better? She agonised that he looked so thin and pale. Did he have any idea, she asked him, how much she worried about him? Did he know that all she did was think of him, wondering where he was and if he was all right?

Although she did not tell James, she was wearing herself out with her concern about the war. She rarely went out, acutely aware that trips to the ballet or opera appeared frivolous at such a time, and anyway she longed to spend the whole evening tucked up in front of the television watching the news. She even welcomed a nasty cold as it allowed her a whole day in bed with constant news bulletins.

She realised that she was becoming more and more introverted, but deep down she felt that it was doing her some good, that, by learning to be with herself, she was growing stronger. She felt lonely, but even that was not so debilitating because she was not alone. She knew that there were thousands of women in the same position, women who were terrified yet were being strong for their men. She felt comforted with that sense of identification.

Of course, most of the time her mind was occupied with James and teeming with memories, but it was also filled with hopes and plans for the future. She did not want to burden him with the pain that she was releasing because she knew that that would be selfish and insensitive when he was going through so much, but she found the courage to examine her fears when she was alone. She felt proud that at last she was no longer running from herself; she was staying with her feelings and learning to handle them. Occasionally she would lapse into a fit of despair when she would cry with great surges of fear and buried angst, but afterwards she would feel relieved, emptied. It was necessary to take the pressure off herself, to defuse the time bomb that she felt was ticking away inside her. She had started to give herself credit for finally trying to understand herself and honour what she wanted.

From her letters, James could sense her struggle and he felt proud of her. Those letters, which sometimes did not arrive for weeks and would then arrive in a great mass, were his lifeline. They kept his morale up. As always he could not share his secret with the men, could not whoop with joy as they did when they received a letter from their wives or girlfriends, but the fact that he could not read bits out aloud did not mean that he did not savour them every bit as much. He read and reread them just as frequently as they did.

In the same way that James could not confide in his men, Diana could not share her anxieties with anyone in her immediate circle except Ken Wharfe and Carolyn Bartholomew, to whom she spoke of James frequently. When Carolyn went off for a couple of weeks on her annual holiday to the Bahamas, Diana was denied even her counsel for a while. What Diana really wanted was to be with James's family in Devon. She knew that they too were worried for James and it was comforting to be able to discuss their fears, to talk openly.

Two weeks after he had left, she drove down to Devon to have lunch and spend the afternoon with Mrs Hewitt and James's sister Syra. Throughout the entire journey down she listened to their favourite Pavarotti tape, remembering how every aria marked a particularly special day. She felt calmer as soon as she turned the bend to the Hewitts' house. Once inside, she found it strange to be in his house without him, but wonderful to be among his family. It was as if she felt both further from him and closer to him all at once.

Their talk was cosy and of James. When you are in love all you want to do is talk about it, and Diana was no exception. It was so liberating not to have to watch herself, to be able to speak freely. She soon found herself openly unleashing her torrent of affection for James. She was delighted to be back in his home; sitting by the fire and giggling with his sister brought back numerous happy memories. They laughed about him, wondering how he was coping without his freshly pressed shirts, his whisky and his regular copies of *Horse and Hound*.

Before she had to leave she went and sat alone in James's bedroom on his bed. There, she could breathe in his atmosphere, the smell of him lingering in the room. She looked with longing at the neat rows of his loafers, their shape kept intact with wooden shoe-trees; she pored over his team photographs and she hugged his pillows to her. She had been through so much, she reflected, in this safe, cosy room with its sloping ceilings and wooden beams. He had been so good to her.

If anything happened to him, she did not know how she would cope.

In his first six weeks in the Gulf, James had to prepare his men for battle. They had to acclimatise themselves to the arduous physical climate, the harsh extremes of temperature, and they had to prepare themselves psychologically. He enjoyed the camaraderie of being part of a team. He felt utterly comfortable with the men, uniting with them as they went through their daily tasks, but, as he was their officer, he knew the importance of remaining perceptibly distant. He could not afford to be too chummy in case group discipline waned, but he had to be approachable.

It was a balance that he was acutely conscious of and never faltered in maintaining. While the prospect of war filled the men with gut-wrenching fear, it brought them together in a silently supportive way that perhaps only war can. As they trained, they bonded as a team, gaining strength from one another.

James had to pull the men together and help them find their own courage. He had to be one step ahead, goading himself on; you cannot lead with fear. As they neared actual battle, their joky, blokish good humour changed. No one had much enthusiasm for the games of rounders in relaxation time; the teasing fell away and their smiles became forced as their fear inevitably increased.

A few days before moving to the central assembly area, the men were given a rousing briefing. They were told that they had to be prepared for the horrific sights and sounds of battle, that they would, indeed, hear people screaming and they would see bodies blown away. Limbs would be torn apart by artillery and lives obliterated in seconds. And some of them, they were warned, would not even live to see such sights.

They were being told this, said their commanding officer, this talk was so bloody, so frank, because they could not afford to shirk the truth. They had to confront what was going to happen or they would be mentally paralysed. They must not thrust it to the backs of their minds but must bring it to the fore and keep it there. Otherwise they would not be able to function, to go into automatic pilot, under the immense pressure. They would be unable to practise their first aid, to relieve trapped bodies as fast as possible and to escape.

As they listened, the reality dawned. They really were going to fight. They might well die and if they did not, they would never be the same again. They might never recover from the trauma. Some men bravely wiped away silent tears of panic at the thought that they might never see their families again, that they might not survive. But however horrible the words that they were hearing, they were grateful. Now at least they knew and they would never look back and say that they had not been warned, had not been prepared as much as they ever could be.

They were told to share their fears, that it was only by articulating them that they would release the personal courage that is a natural element in us all. But they must awaken their courage in time, and the only way that they could bring it to the fore was by discussing their terror, not by keeping it in. They could, at least, all have complete confidence in their professionalism, they were told, because they were all consummate professionals. They were superbly trained and just had to let their talents flourish. They had an awesome responsibility ahead of them, but their superiors had no doubts that they would live up to what was required of them.

As James listened to this moving speech, he had no thoughts for Diana, no thoughts for anything other than his duty. He had to focus on his men. There was a monumental task ahead; it was going to be a vile, bloody war. Later, as they had their usual Sunday service and whispered their pre-battle prayers, he knew that he did not want to die. All the men looked forward to this service, to the encouraging words of the regimental padre. They were comforted by the prayers, by standing in front of the small trestle table covered with an altar cloth. It did not matter that they were standing in the middle of the desert, so exposed, singing their hymns; they still felt that God was with them, that he was on their side, and they prayed as they had never prayed before.

As he sang 'Onward, Christian Soldiers' and 'The Lord Is My Shepherd', joining with his men's dull monotone, the sand blowing up around his feet, James felt almost ashamed that he had thought that he wanted to die. Now he could not afford to think about himself; he had to think only of his men. He was proud of their bravery, moved that they could stand here singing in the face of death. He had to live in order to try to ensure that they return safely to their families. That was his job and he would do all he could to fulfil it.

James repeatedly told his men that they had to remember what they were fighting for, and that they had to keep their sights on their return home. He urged each of them to have a pleasant goal in his mind to keep him going, whether it was his first pint in the local pub or being in the arms of his loved ones. They must never forget their motivation. Certainly he knew what he was living for. However hard he had tried to convince himself that it was not the case, he yearned to return to Diana.

Back in England, Diana was praying too. Ever since she had started to allow her emotions a freer rein, she had found herself turning to the Church. She realised that to find the inner peace she desired so badly she had to have some support, and she discovered that her quest was facilitated by regular trips to the altar rail.

She was beginning to see that the process of healing had to do with acceptance. She knew that she could not change the past, so she had to learn to let go of it. If she truly wanted peace she had to surrender. She had to trust God, and to say over and over, 'Thy will be done.' She had to release the force of her own will.

Ever since she was a young girl, she had found chapels soothing. She had spent many hours sitting in the private chapel at Althorp when she had felt fraught and miserable. She had always thought how lucky she was that her family had its own chapel, that all they had to do was enter that blessed room to the right at the top of the stairs and immediately they would be calmed. She would perch on one of the small wooden pews, beneath the towering stained-glass window, and let peace and calm envelop her.

Lately she had gained real solace from the Church. Sitting in chapels, she found that her communication with the higher force was so much easier, so much clearer, and as she was growing spiritually, the unspoken call was getting louder. She was increasingly drawn to Catholicism and High Anglicanism. The protective club that Catholics form appealed to her, especially as two of her closest girlfriends were staunch Catholics. Through the Honourable Rosa Monckton and Lucia Flecha de Lima, the wife of the Brazilian Ambassador then in London, Diana learned that the structure of Catholicism is much firmer than that of the Church of England. She discovered that that rigid structure requires greater discipline and that it is through discipline that one can increase one's feeling of self-worth and eventually gain peace.

As often as she could, Diana would creep into churches and light a candle for James. She felt closer to him during church services, particularly at the Guards Chapel near Buckingham Palace where she knew his regiment had prayed. As often as possible, she would dart up the wide steps and slip into the back of the modern chapel for Sunday morning prayers. At times like those, when she wanted to be alone with God and her thoughts, she dearly hoped that she would not be noticed. She did not want those sacred moments violated by prying eyes. She needed to be quiet, to think and to pray.

Sometimes, she thought that she would burst with the desire to be normal. She craved to do normal things and to leave the drama and the panic behind. She could feel the frustration bubbling within that, even when she was on her knees in that sacred space, heads would be surreptitiously turning and she could feel people's eyes boring into her back. She felt suffocated by the lack of pure air that was allowed to circulate around her; the only air that she was permitted to breathe was air sullied with other people's whispers. It was then that she turned her thoughts to the heavens and prayed that one day her wish for freedom would be granted.

Weekends were the most difficult. She found herself dreading them as they dragged endlessly and she felt lost and lonely. She did not want to go to Highgrove and did not dare leave Kensington Palace for long in case, by some miracle, James might call. He had managed to telephone late one Saturday night and hearing his voice had changed the whole tempo of her day. He had given her the most enormous lift. Just to know that he was all right, that he was thinking of her, made her heart sing.

Most of the time she stayed in London alone. She had become increasingly solitary, rarely seeing her friends, and her sense of isolation prompted her mind to run wild. All she could do was to think of James and to worry. When she had not heard any news of him for a while, she would send herself frantic with the careless train of her thoughts. Not knowing for sure whether he was still alive was almost impossible to cope with. If only, she wished, if only she just had a return date to hold on to, to pin her hopes on, she would be able to manage. The vacuum of the unknown ahead of her, the empty space that either threatened the worst or was filled with the ecstasy of his homecoming, wore her out.

One Sunday she decided to brave an outing and, as William was away at school, took Harry to lunch with some friends near Wantage. It was an idyllic scene – a happily married couple in a beautiful house with two children scampering around. While Diana enjoyed the day, while it felt so good to be with such happy, normal people, she returned home feeling low and vulnerable. It was so sad, she thought: all she had ever wanted was so simple; what she had tasted that day was all she had ever prayed for.

The only weekends that she really enjoyed were those she spent in Devon when she went to stay with Mrs Hewitt. Then she felt safe and that she could let herself go a little. She could ease her strain by sharing her anxieties with Shirley Hewitt who was so kind and understanding. It was important to her to go, and she felt that her visits were special and valuable; they all needed each other at this time. Often she would take Harry as he loved the horses in the stable yard and liked to hear about James. To a much lesser degree than his mother he too was obsessed by the war; he was turning into quite a little soldier, even going to bed dressed in full combat kit.

The weekdays were not so torturous as those grim weekends in Kensington Palace, as at least she had her work to keep her mind occupied. However busy she was, though, however late she returned to Kensington Palace, she never failed to write to James. She could not bear the thought that her letters were not reaching him and once rang the post office, and then the Officers' Mess at Windsor, to see how long they were taking to arrive.

She told James that she had the strongest feelings that he was very lonely inside and she wanted to reiterate that he was not alone. She loved him and was behind him and was so terribly proud of him and all the men. She said that she knew that he would be furious, that he would not approve, but she had had his astrological chart done. She had rung up his mother to find out what time he had been born and been to see an astrologer who had spotted his loneliness. Diana had been worried but, trying to keep her tone as light as she knew he would like, she told James that he should take heart because his leadership qualities were prominent and they were excellent. He was born to lead and he must remember that people recognised what a strong and special person he was.

Diana really tried her hardest to keep the pain that never left her from her pen. All she wanted to do was to make James's task more bearable, to reassure him that he was supported and adored. She was delighted, she said, that finally she had been given a real opportunity to help: she had been granted permission to go and visit the wives of the troops in Germany. She had such a wish to be with them, to comfort them, as she knew exactly what they were going through. She knew that they must be tormenting themselves, because she certainly was.

When she visited a leprosy mission in Cambridge, somebody asked Diana why she was so thin. She told them that it was all the exercise that she was taking, but really it was the worry. The vigilant watch that she kept up day and night, praying for James's safety, was exhausting her. It had wiped all the fun, all the spontaneity, clean out of her. All she felt was tired and serious.

She told James as much as she could, in easy code, about how terrible things were for her at the Palace. She had to keep herself physically fit, she stressed, because psychologically she was confused. She could sense that she was surrounded by a lot of people who were jealous of her and out to get her. The atmosphere was electric and she felt as if she needed to have eyes in the back of her head. She knew that she could not afford to relax or she would be crucified. But the agony of waiting to hear from him, the sheer terror of not knowing how he was, she said, was worse than anything she had ever been through. This was by far the most difficult thing she had ever had to endure.

Diana, whose every breath seemed to her to be documented, could not believe that the truth about Charles and his relationship with Camilla Parker-Bowles had not become public knowledge. She felt hurt that people had not sensed her desperation. It made her quite frantic that no one had seen her grief and tried to help her. Yet she had been patient; intuitively she knew that the truth will out, and she had waited.

The spiritual advisers she had consulted had told her over and over that once she fulfilled her duty she would be granted the happiness she craved, that the separation that she longed for would come about. Diana had believed them in the past because she had needed to. But now she instinctively felt more confident; she believed that the end was in sight. She knew that the media bubble would burst as relations between her and Charles were dangerously bad. A weekend with him at Highgrove had confirmed that they found it unbearable to be under the same roof, let alone in the same room. Diana knew that she could no longer stomach the deception. She had lost the will to fight; it was like pushing a boulder up a steep hill and she no longer had the energy.

Just as James and Diana had an emotionally giving relationship, they had also always showered each other with gifts, tokens of their love. Diana had bought James shirts and jumpers on birthdays and at Christmas and other odd moments to thank him for being with her, for supporting her. She had always been touched that James would regularly arrive to see her with a bunch of white lilies in his hand or a bottle of her favourite scent. He gave her items of clothing that she had borrowed when she was staying in Devon and was eager to keep – his cricket jersey and a Puffa jacket. He had long promised her, though, that if she stopped biting her nails, he would buy her something really special.

Before he left for the Gulf, he had bought her an expensive pair of emerald and diamond earrings which had then got lost in the post at Kensington Palace. He was devastated when he heard that she had not received them, and Ken Wharfe was dispatched to sort the matter out. Eventually the small package was located, and when Diana opened it she was thrilled. She was overwhelmed that he should spoil her so and wrote to thank him and to tell him that her nails were in excellent order, that she spent hours painting them bright red so that if he should ever catch a glimpse of a picture of her, he would see for himself.

From her letters, James could detect Diana's growing sense of self. She seemed to be gaining in strength as she believed in herself more and did not seem so frightened by life. Certainly she was tackling her work with a new confidence. Her interest in AIDS had not waned and she told James that she planned to give a big speech. She said that he would probably find that surprising as he knew how much she loathed public speaking, but this subject was important to her and she wanted to bring it wider recognition. She had been at a grand reception at the House of Commons for an AIDS charity and had quite impressed herself that conversationally she had managed to hold her own with the many MPs to whom she had spoken. It was a subject that she felt proud to know so much about, and increasing knowledge gave her a harder edge, a stronger corner from which to fight the Palace over the issue of her charity work: at least they could not simply dismiss her with a quick flick – as though she were irrelevant – as they had tried to in the past.

She may not have won her battle with Charles to go and visit

the troops in the Gulf, but at least she was going to Germany –
to James's very camp – to spend eight hours with the officers'
wives at Sennelager and Paderborn. She had fought hard to go
out to the Gulf, not just because of the *frisson* of anticipation that
she might even see James, but because she was genuinely proud
of and wanted to support the British troops. As she herself knew,
no visitor could boost morale quite in the way she could, and
she smiled to herself that few were aware of the comprehensive
knowledge of the situation that she had gained. She had both
a personal insight from James and a public one from watching
back-to-back news reports. But the Palace had refused her,
saying that she would distract attention from Charles. He
must go, they had said stiffly, as he needed to be seen there;
he needed the support. Seething with silent fury, Diana had
given in. What was the use? She knew that the Palace was
closing round Prince Charles fast and tight. The drawbridge
was coming down – and where would she be?

10

Nothing boosted morale for the men out in the Gulf as much as receiving letters from home. It was the vital contact that they needed to remind them what they were fighting for, and what they had to look forward to on their return. Diana may have been the most prolific of James's correspondents but she was not alone in writing to him. As well as his family, who sent regular letters, he found that friends who were thinking about him and were concerned for him would occasionally write. Some took him by surprise as he had not heard from them for a long time.

One such correspondent was a former girlfriend, Emma Stewardson, with whom James had had possibly his most serious relationship before he had met Diana. Their relationship had fizzled out, as most of his relationships had, with Emma walking away because she could not get James to meet her level of commitment. As soon as a hint of true intimacy had come into the equation, he had backed off. His fear had hurt Emma, who had thought that they were destined to share their lives. Sensing her wishes and knowing that he was not ready – silently wondering if he would ever be ready – James had rejected her with his passivity. It was the very fact that he did not put up a fight when she threatened to leave him, and that he had no answer when she said that what he was offering was not enough, that had said it all. Emma had left him, but she had not forgotten him.

When she heard that he had gone to fight in the Gulf, she allowed her feelings for him to rekindle. After all, nobody had touched her heart the way he had, and maybe, she thought, just maybe there was still a chance. James was truly glad to hear from her, glad to know that he was in as many people's thoughts as possible while he was stranded in the desert. He wrote back and for the first time with her he was unguarded. What did it matter what he wrote when every letter might be his last? Certainly the distance from home and the uncertainty of war heightened everyone's emotions. So he was a little more generous with his feelings towards her than he had been before, and he promised more than he ever intended to fulfil.

It came as a shock to Emma, therefore, to read in a gossip column that James was also receiving regular letters from the Princess of Wales. She was hurt and she wanted revenge. She sold her story of her affair with James to a Sunday newspaper.

James was passed a copy of the newspaper out in the desert and read the piece with incredulity. It seemed surreal to be reading about yourself in this way, so alone and so cut off from all the people who had already seen it. Like the gossip-column item that Emma had read, but which James had been unaware of, it included mention of Diana writing letters and sending gifts to him in the Gulf. As he scanned the pages, his eyes racing over the words before he had time to take them in, he was seized by an impotent rage.

Perhaps if he had just been dealing with anger, if he had only had to absorb the acrid taste of betrayal, he could have coped better. He could have channelled the fumes of his emotion into his work and kept himself too occupied to notice their escape. He could have dismissed Emma with a fit of fury and closed his mind to the episode for good.

Unfortunately the situation was more complicated. This was the moment he had been dreading more than death. That he had been expecting it for so long did not prevent the panic and fear from shooting through him. For now that their secret was out there would be no peace. His life would never be the same. That the papers had news of his and Diana's friendship meant that from now on he would be a target. Whatever he did he could not win. He would be written off because no one would know the truth, would understand their situation.

The wretched paper that he held in his hands was a brittle

reminder that everyone with whom he had associated was now caught up in this world of public gossip. They were targets too. Now that they were of interest, some of them were, no doubt, feeling self-important. It was shameful but it was true.

He felt a deep and unfamiliar sense of insecurity. Would people no longer like him for what he was, only who he was? Would he ever be able to enjoy unconditional friendship again? Would he no longer be able to trust anyone? It was sad, he thought, that he would have to coat himself with cynicism, that he could no longer afford to offer open, honest friendship to all. Now he would have to doubt first, to test before he could let go.

It reminded him of one of Diana's recent letters. Now, he knew what she was talking about first hand. It was so sad, she had written, that everybody in her world had to be tarred with the same brush, that they had to be exposed because of their association with her. It was so unfair that unwittingly she dragged those she loved through the line of fire. She was referring to her younger brother, Charles, whom she had always adored and remained close to. He had had a brief affair one weekend in Paris with a fashionable figure called Sally Ann Lasson, shortly after his marriage to model Victoria Lockwood.

The papers had got hold of it, Diana told James, because Sally Ann had decided to squeal, and Charles had been under siege. He had rung her up apologising for the fuss, and all Diana had felt was overwhelming pity for him and livid frustration at her position. That her brother had made a mistake and should now have to pay for it in front of the world hurt Diana deeply. Far from feeling any shame from the situation, she felt nothing but sympathy. She knew where her loyalties lay: her own family came first. She had given up trying to maintain appearances for the sake of the Crown.

Fortunately James could not focus on the anxiety that he felt. The newspapers in England had got hold of the fact that Diana was writing to him. They knew that she was sending him the cigarettes, sweets and batteries that he had asked her to send, as well as food hampers from Fortnum and Mason, and Turnbull and Asser shirts. He was relieved that he did not have much time to attend to the worry that this fomented in him, because he had to give all his energies to the war. He could not dwell on his own problems; he had another battle to fight that was far more important, and at least he was prepared for that one and had the right weapons. He had nothing to fight his personal battle with; there were no weapons that would be of any use.

In his rare quiet moments he wondered who could have told the papers. He never found out. He had always been slightly worried by Diana's friendship with Major David Waterhouse and it was he who came under James's suspicion. David Waterhouse, the debonair nephew of the Duke of Marlborough, was also out in the Gulf with the Life Guards and perhaps, thought James, he was jealous that he was not receiving so much attention from the Princess.

Ever since Diana had been photographed with Waterhouse at a David Bowie pop concert in 1987, after she had met him through the Duchess of York, James had been jealous of their friendship. That the press had made far too much of it, omitting to mention that Princess Margaret's son, Viscount Linley, had also been present at the concert, standing the other side of Diana, had done little to quell James's worst fears. Diana had repeatedly tried to reassure James, telling him over and over that she and David were just friends.

Now she reiterated it more than ever in her letters. She could not bear it that James was so upset and that he was so far from her. She wrote to say that she was sure David was just making mischief, that really James had to believe that nothing had ever happened between them, that she did not love anybody as much as she loved him and that she was fiercely protective of him. She worried that she sounded like a clucking hen in her letters, but she was always so anxious for him.

James was so terrified that their secret was already leaking out, and that his future would be tarnished with disapproval, that nothing that she wrote would placate him. The fear of battle, the bombs and the lives that he had seen lost had not frightened him as much as this, for now he felt sure that his days with Diana were numbered.

Because he suspected that there could be no future, that their love was never meant to exist exposed, he started to withdraw. He had prepared himself mentally before to leave her and he would do so again. It was so much harder the second time around, he thought, because he knew how difficult the separation would be. That he had faced the misery before and survived meant nothing. Now he had the dreary prospect of facing it again – and this time he knew that he would have to suffer for longer, possibly for ever.

Diana was thrilled to receive his call, but quickly felt frantic. James's usual tones of glee at hearing her voice were dimmed. All that she could detect was a chill of concern. His voice was taut, strained with anxiety, as he asked her what the situation was in England. What were people saying about them? Diana attempted to set his mind at rest, telling him that the story had died down, that this should not come between them. She tried to cheer him up by asking where he was and said that after she had put the telephone down she would rush straight to the map and locate him.

In fact her mood was leaden when she had finished talking to him. She liked to think that she had found a route to him, a way through his emotional isolation so that she could always reach him. Yet he had been so distant. She tried to put it down to his fear, but – what if he left her now? What if he could not bear the attention, could not stand the infamy and walked away? She knew that he had had to pay a high price to stay with her; what if he could no longer pay it?

She found herself listening to her opera tapes, and the mournful passion of the music produced heart-rending loneliness. She would listen to the Irish singer Sinéad O'Connor's haunting love song 'Nothing Compares 2 U' and weep with the strain of being alone. She was worn out, weary from the effort of loving when she did not know where it was taking her, when she did not know what the answers were. All she knew was that blindly she would go on. She could not mitigate the obsession of missing James, of wanting him.

Again, prayer was her salvation. Every night, and as often as she thought of him through the day, she prayed for his safe return. She was gaining such strength from her faith that she felt sure that whatever happened, it would be right. After all, she was learning to let go. She felt heady with relief that she had given Prince Charles her ultimatums. She was so proud that she had asserted herself, that she had told him plainly that something had to be done about their marriage. Now she felt that she had done all she could, and she must sit back and watch.

The last thing she had ever wanted was for her marriage to have to end and, while she felt that she would only be free of the weight of the trauma when it did, the romantic core of her never let go of her dream. Although she could not rid herself of the vile pull of hate for Charles, it was as if there was always a tiny reminder that the ultimate hatred is so clear and pure that it is only a wisp away from love. She may have been too proud to acknowledge it but even in the grip of her hatred, she longed for him to come to her, to beg her forgiveness, and for them to try again.

Which is why, when the media bubble burst on the Duchess of York who wanted a separation from Prince Andrew – something that Diana had predicted to James would happen – Diana did not join the Duchess there and then in distancing herself from the royal family. It was not just her need to remain close to her boys that kept her back, not just her desire to groom William for his role, but the frail thread of hope of which she could not let go.

As Diana watched Sarah try to break away, as she heard the reprimands echo through the Palace, she felt no envy for her. She did not want to halt her own course of action – she knew that she could not, because together she and Charles were on an inexorable downward slide – but nevertheless she feared for Sarah. Temporarily it was preferable, as she heard the distant roar of thunder, to be cowering in the shade rather than standing in the full swell of the storm.

Diana and Sarah had never been close, but now Sarah needed her as an ally and as a shoulder to lean on. Only an insider knew how bad it could be; only someone who had rammed her head against the palace walls knew how inflexible and unyielding they were; only an outsider who had married in knew how lonely you could feel, how unnourished as duty came before emotion every time.

Diana knew and she understood. She was at the end of the telephone and she was as supportive as possible as she received Sarah's anxious calls. At the same time she was happier in herself. She had had a call from James and, having heard the right signs in his voice, was replenished. The old endearments were back and she felt sure that everything was going to be all right between them. Because she felt chirpier and calmer, she felt stronger. Unlike Sarah, she would wait. She would bide her time in the misguided belief that thereby she would earn some sort of justice.

Diana knew that she had acquired a lot of much-needed strength, but she felt as if she had weights strapped to her feet as she tried to plough on through royal life. The more she tried to make a stand, the more firmly the Palace resisted her. She was being throttled, but now she had the will to keep fighting.

She refused to go skiing with Charles as she thought such activities smacked of flippancy and insouciance while British troops were fighting in the Gulf. What frustrated Diana beyond belief was that the Palace thought that every decision she made was calculated to win some kind of publicity war against her husband. Of course, she could not tell them that she cared deeply about the men in the Gulf, that she was breathless with concern for one man in particular, but the fact that they refused to take her seriously both infuriated and insulted her.

Still they saw her as the spoilt problem child. Still it was she who received the blunt edge of their hostility, not Camilla Parker-Bowles who she felt was surely to blame for her marital troubles. That the Queen accepted Mrs Parker-Bowles, that she welcomed her into her home, was a slap in the face for Diana.

If they wanted to negate her, to delete Diana from their view, they could not have done it more beautifully.

However, Diana was learning to match them. In her quiet way she had kept her eyes open for such a long time that she had learned their ways; they had trapped her in the royal maze for over a decade, so by now she could find her way straight to the centre. She declined Charles's offer to hold a big party that coming July to celebrate her thirtieth birthday and her tenth wedding anniversary. She knew that that was what the Palace wanted, that it would make Charles appear the caring, generous husband, but it was too late for that now. She would no longer be a party to the lies. She wanted to lift the lid on the deception that had corroded her spirit. Prince Charles was furious. He was unaccustomed to her new, cool defiance. It was more unnerving than the fits of hysteria which he had been able to dismiss. Secretly it frightened him as he did not know which way she would turn next.

It sickened Diana that Charles's advisers had suggested that he spend more time with the boys, that he must uphold the image of the concerned family man, the loving father.

She was so proud when she looked at her boys; to see them growing up was a constant reminder that in one sphere at least she had not failed. She had often had to drag every ounce of energy out of herself to appear stable and normal in front of them, but she knew that she had done her very best. Whenever her self-esteem was flagging, she had only to look at her sons to know that in this one area she had succeeded. She was bursting with pride that William was maturing into his role, and that discussions were under way about her taking him to Cardiff for St David's Day. She longed to show him off.

She would never deny the children time with their father because she knew that they needed that crucial male bonding. While she tried her hardest to keep the acid out of her tone when she spoke about Prince Charles in front of them, it cut her to the quick when they had left her and again she was alone. The isolation was numbing. If only she could share their triumphs with an involved, caring partner. Her greatest desire had been to watch them grow up with her husband beside her so that their foundations would be rooted in the security of united pride. Such thoughts reminded her of the times when she and James had leaned against the white fence at Highgrove and cheered as Harry had jumped his first jumps on his pony; and when, amidst splashes and laughter, they had applauded the boys as they raced each other in the swimming pool.

She did not want William and Harry to mature with the taint of fear and uncertainty as they watched their parents together, wondering what would happen next. She could not bear to see their dear, trusting faces and stiff, hesitant little bodies as they saw her approach their father. She tried to be supple and relaxed with him, but children are so dangerously aware, so much more difficult to deceive than adults.

It had been mooted that Diana might visit India, but she postponed her trip as she did not want to go anywhere during the Gulf War. If the truth be known, she told James, she did not want to go away for fear of missing his calls. Anyway, she was still getting a tremendous amount of satisfaction from her work in England. She wrote to him after a visit to a hospice, telling him that she had practically sobbed her way around. It had been dreadfully emotionally harrowing as there had been so many ill and dying people, but the visit had given her a feeling of self-worth. As she sat by beds, drinking in the fear of the sick, she knew that she could be of help because she could relate. Pain was a subject that she had much to say about. She had reached the stage, she told James, where futile dinner-party conversation bored her as she could no longer identify with what seemed the petty concerns of her old friends. What did it matter where you went for your holidays, what the smartest restaurants were, when inside you were hurting? To be in beautiful places alone merely intensified the pain. No, she assured James, these days she enjoyed visiting the homeless more than listening to idle party gossip.

When the news came that Kuwait had been liberated, that Iraq's army was defeated, Diana felt as though she would collapse with relief. She knew that it was not a time for euphoria, that it was not a time to gloat, but it was a time for pride. Tears trickled down her face as she watched President Bush's rousing speech on the news. She was not just crying for herself, crying with relief that the strain was over, but she was crying for the country. She was crying for the mothers who had lost their brave sons, for the wives who had lost their husbands, the women who had lost their lovers and the children who had lost their fathers. It had been a terrible three months and the nation was exhausted, but there had been dignity in the struggle and the country had been united. Now, at least, spirits could rise as people prepared to welcome their heroes home, although there was an eternity ahead for the dead to be mourned.

Diana kept writing to James since she knew that the fact that a ceasefire had come into force did not mean that the troops would be on the next plane home. There was still much work to be done.

She continued to send James letters of support. She told him how cherished he was; she worried that he must be feeling shocked and exhausted and she promised him his heart's desire when he returned home. She teased him about the moustache that he had grown during battle, saying that she hoped it was removed before she set eyes on him as she was sure that she would hate it. She wanted him as clean-cut as ever.

James flew back to Germany with his men. He wanted to savour the warm regimental welcome with his soldiers. He was escorted out of the back exit of the aeroplane and taken in a staff car to the barracks, because he was determined to avoid the photographers who had gathered to snap him. He did not want this day marred, as he knew that the rest were bound to be. He wanted to taste the triumph with his men, to slap them on the back with pride and watch with eyes wet with emotion as they fell into the arms of their families back at the camp. The band played, banners were waved and he knew that it was a day he would never forget. Perhaps he would never feel the charge of such high emotion again; he might never again see grown men drop their guard and cry with the relief of having returned, with the joy of being alive.

*   *   *

The next day he flew back to England and went straight to Highgrove. Diana had arranged for a member of her staff to meet him half-way and bundle him into the boot of the car so that nobody would see his arrival. They did not want the reunion that they had been waiting for, that they had both been living for, to be denigrated by wagging tongues or, worse, by photographers. They were both trembling with anticipation. The adrenalin of war was still coursing through James's veins. He had not had time to stop and let go. The fear, the sorrow, the elation and the protracted build-up of exhaustion were still locked up inside him; he was still firing on all cylinders, unaware that they were empty of fuel.

The moment he saw Diana standing in the drawing room waiting for him, they were in each other's arms. Neither knew how they had so quickly and efficiently found their way to each other; they only knew that with all the tension that they had endured they were ready to explode. They were tense not just from the separation, the terrible wait and the disjointed communication, but from the fear of the future. Now that the press was aware of their friendship, they did not know what was going to happen. They knew that they had to be even more careful than before and that the pressure would be worse.

None of this was spoken as they lay locked together, breathing one breath. They had so much to catch up on that they did not dare begin. They did not know if they had the strength or the words to express what they had each gone through which, each in its own way, had been so traumatic.

And anyway there was plenty of time. They had the whole clear expanse of their future ahead, like the calm sea leading to the horizon. Yet, much as they both wanted it, neither deluded themselves that this was really the case. James had known for a long time that their love was the stuff of magic, that it was a fairy tale that could exist only as myth and not as reality. As long as Diana had believed that they had a future, he had kept the dream going, kept it alive to please and to nourish her.

Now, as she lay against him and his body took her weight, he could feel her doubt. He sensed that suddenly she had faced the truth. His shock was unendurable; he felt paralysed with grief, with the knowing and now the realisation that the moment had come. He did not know when she had known, but he suspected that the moment she had seen him, she had known that it could not last.

She had had to believe it while he was away. Her reveries had kept her sane, her dreams that he would return and they would live together, that they would throw open the doors on their private heaven and let real life in. But now he was here and she was frightened. This was real; this chest that she leaned against was solid. It was what she had been waiting for, but what she had been waiting for was a dream. It was a dream that now she too knew could never come true.

They lay weeping in each other's arms. They were too afraid to confront each other with the real reason for their tears. They both knew, but they both pretended that they were tears of relief. They kept up the façade when really they were both feeling totally desolate. They both knew that grand passion does not have a happy end, that the love that they had felt had been so overpowering that it could not last. It had survived amid the secrecy and doubt, and now when it might be truly aired they were afraid. It was not the idea of exposure that crippled them, more the fear that what they had was too beautiful to withstand the everyday routine of living. It was so powerful that it was too fragile to sustain reality. They had been swept up in a dream, and now that the cold light of day was upon them, they knew that together they would freeze to death.

Implicity they understood that if they stayed together their feelings would become mediocre, and great love is not about the mediocre. It is about grand passion and great loss. It was as if only by ending their romance could they keep it alive. They were too afraid to risk anything more; they could not bear to go on and kill it.

James left Diana the next morning overwrought and exhausted. There had been no explanations, no real talk, yet the message was clear. She was not going to fight any more, to take any more chances. She no longer needed his support enough to risk losing everything. She had found her strength and now she was ready to walk slowly away. It had had to happen. It would not be a clean break; it would be slow and suffocating. She would keep up just enough contact to keep him hanging on, to give him hope.

He had never forced his unhappiness on her and he was not about to start now. He would nurse his wounds alone, and would smile bravely whenever he saw her so as not to disappoint her.

When James had had time to simmer down, when he had let the trauma of war seep from his bones and he had slept out his bitter disappointment, he began trying to put things into perspective. All he could think of was Diana and the love that they had shared. He was consumed with her and in his agony he could feel the first flickers of anger. He read and reread the letters that she had sent him, the fat bundle that she had urged him to destroy, and, as the words of her promises leapt at him, he felt a surge of injustice. If only they had had the time to find their natural course. If the press had not found out about them, if the stakes had not been raised so high, perhaps they would have worked things out together. As it was, Diana had withdrawn. Now she was too busy to see him; she had made another life in which he appeared to play no part. He felt bitterly rejected and alone. And, if he could bear to face it, he felt used.

He was aware that he had worked hard for her, that he had risked everything to make her happy, to keep her going. But now that she was tougher, she might well reap the rewards with another man. Now that she was sophisticated and worldly and even more beautiful, she was slipping from his grasp.

What he did not see was that it was not just him that Diana was turning from. It was as if in a bid to build her strength further, in her quest to find her own life, she was retreating from her past in every sense. As she was growing, her friends were changing. Instead of remaining close to her comfortable old friends who really loved her and had only ever wanted to help her, suddenly she seemed to have found her way into a more mature, glamorous circle. How could her new friends, such as the Honourable Rosa Monckton and the indefatigably social Lady Palumbo, have seen the point of a man like James Hewitt? He was neither rich nor intellectual. They would not have known that he was a kind, loyal man who had helped Diana become the woman they saw and admired, that he had helped her pick up the pieces of her broken life and that together they had painstakingly welded them back together.

James, like many of Diana's other friends, had been approached by the press. When these friends had gone to Diana and asked what to do, she had replied nebulously, 'Do what you think best.' James had not spoken, but others equally loyal, such as Carolyn Bartholomew, had. At first Diana had been pleased with the reaction. She had been relieved that the world had at last been made aware of the shocking truth about her marriage and her bulimia. She was undoubtedly helped by the exposure.

But she was also trapped. Suddenly she was not seen as the coolly elegant princess with the Midas touch; she was seen for what she was, a desperate and lonely young woman. She was no longer as dignified and aloof and she never would be again. A part of her felt diminished by the world's knowledge of the truth, and she knew that the repercussions of this blast of honesty would affect her profoundly. The country was in an uproar over the shattered state of the monarchy and the Palace laid the blame firmly at her door.

Diana withdrew and distanced herself from her old circle. James may not have played any part in the revelations but he had been the pivotal character in her life. He had witnessed her metamorphosis as he had helped to remove her unhappiness. Diana felt that if she was truly to turn the corner, if she was to embrace a new life, she would have to leave him behind.

11

James was hurting as he had never hurt in his life before, and the pain was physical. It gripped him deep in his stomach and on some days he was out of breath with it. It seemed so difficult to be mourning the lost love of someone who was alive, and often he wondered if it would be easier if Diana was dead. Then at least he would know that he could never repeat that love; eventually, he might learn to accept his fate.

But this way was so cruel. She was alive and he could not turn round without seeing her. Her every move was documented, every smile kept alive by the camera, so how could he even begin to shut her out? And every day he just could not rid himself of the thought that there was always the distant chance that she would come to him again. He was numb with agony and self-loathing. The pain was so bad that he wanted to make it worse. He had to put an end to his misery somehow and, if he really tried, perhaps he could totally self-destruct.

On the darkest days he could not push away the thought that he had been used, that he had served his purpose and then been dismissed. Now Diana was strong, and he was on his knees.

To torture himself further, he tried to tell himself that if it had not been him it would have been someone else. She had been ready for help, needful of affection, and the next man who had come along would have done the job just as well. But in his heart he knew that that was not true. It had been their destiny to meet. He had loved her for ever, it seemed, from long before they had ever met; it was as if his whole life had been a preparation for this experience.

Diana knew this as well. She could not let him go. However much she tried she could not dismiss James from her thoughts.

She was not strong enough to effect a final break so she kept up a lingering contact. When she felt alone or afraid, it was still to James that she turned.

That June, Prince William was accidentally hit on the head with a golf club at Ludgrove School. Diana was told of the accident while she was lunching at San Lorenzo and immediately rushed to his side. Throughout the whole journey from the Royal Berkshire Hospital, in Reading, where he had first been taken, to London's Great Ormond Street Hospital she was sick with panic. Trying to keep the hysteria from her voice, she soothed William, holding his hand and willing the journey to end.

As soon as they got to the hospital and he was in safe hands, she rang James. She needed support herself and she knew that no one would be calmer or more comforting. It was mid-afternoon and James was at the barracks in Windsor. He could hear the fear and desperation in her voice and was afraid for her. Carefully he told her that he was there for her, that she must relax as he was sure that William was being looked after superbly. He was positive that William was going to be all right; after all, he was a brave, sturdy chap. She must let go now, he told her. She could not afford to wear herself out, must keep her spirits up for William's sake. She had done her best and now there was nothing more that she could do. She could only wait and pray.

Diana was crying, wailing that she feared for William's health so, that she loved him so very dearly and could not bear the thought that anything serious might happen to him, that she could not contemplate life without both her boys' being healthy and happy. She groaned that she had never felt more distraught, more terrified than she did now, that she longed to take the pain from William, that she would do anything to be on the operating table herself and spare him this. James listened, as he had listened in the past, and, when he could, reiterated the soothing words she needed to hear.

As soon as he detected the lilt of panic in her voice subsiding, he told her to go and enquire about William again and made her promise to keep him informed. Diana put down the telephone and, as she walked back up the hospital corridor, she felt the old waves of loneliness wash over her like nausea. It was typical that Charles was not here, just typical that she was dealing with this fear and trauma alone. Suddenly she missed James desperately again. She wanted him with her, wanted his steady arm around her.

She was slipping and she needed him to ground her, to prevent her fall. So she rang him at frequent intervals, from the hospital or from her car outside. She was furious with Charles, she told him; nothing had changed and as usual she was on her own. That he had not cancelled his trip to the opera to be with her had hurt her desperately. It had made her realise that she had been mistaken in thinking that she was untouchable where Charles was concerned. She told James gravely that Charles still had the ability to tear her apart and that the vulnerability he uncovered both frightened and disappointed her.

James understood exactly what she was saying because he felt the same about her. Every time he heard Diana's voice he was set back. He knew that he would have to pay for the joy of hearing her, that afterwards the ache of missing her would be far worse than before. Every time he felt the slightest bit stronger, just when he had managed to convince himself as best he could that he had the potential for life without her, she would contact him and his resolve would crack.

That summer he returned to Germany. It felt appropriate to be back, as that was where he had felt so unhappy before. As he walked the streets of Sennelager, he was soon weighed down with the old misery.

It was the first time in his life that he had truly felt that there was no hope, that however valiantly he tried, he could not rouse himself from his depression. He felt as if he would never feel normal again, never feel the spontaneous bubble of a giggle rise up inside him, was sure that from now on his laughter would always be forced. He presumed that he would wear this misery for ever like a thick outer skin, for how could he hope to shed it? He was only in his early thirties yet he felt that he had done all the living that he ever would. Life would be a slow death from now on.

He consoled himself that at least he had the Army. He had his men. Army life was what he had always wanted and he had to focus on that now. What he had experienced had been the pinnacle of his existence; he had climbed to the summit and he would never forget the view; but now it was over.

As he lay in his plain, bleak flat in Sennelager, he spent hours wondering whether it was better to have had your eyes opened as he had or to walk your life partially blind. Was it preferable to have shared a bond of love with someone and to have felt truly whole, or to spend your life alone not realising how lonely you could be? He knew that there was a price for everything and that he had had so much – far more than most people ever would; but facing the future, accepting the fact that he would spend the rest of his life paying for it, was not easy. In fact it was a form of hell.

It frightened him that he was so unhappy that he could not concentrate on the studies that were so important to his career. He felt so frustrated and emotionally confused that his attention was muddled. Every time he opened a book the pages were blank; all he could see was her. So it came as little surprise to him when he failed his exams for entry to staff training college. He had failed his first army hurdle and he was left feeling even lower and more depleted than before. Now that his career was in jeopardy, that the rise he had been promised was not going to be as swift as he had anticipated, he sank more deeply into despair.

The only light, the first glint of hope, was that he was leaving Germany and was to be stationed at Knightsbridge Barracks again. At least he would not feel so isolated in England. Perhaps he could start to live some sort of life again after all. How ironic, he thought, that now he would be where Diana had always wanted him to be and it was too late. Her letters to the Gulf had been full of her prayers that when he returned he would be stationed in London. She had said that it would be so exciting to have him near her and she had even wondered whether he would stay in the Army. It would have been too much to hope for that he would leave, leave the Army to be free for her.

It was macabre that in the end all her wishes were granted. It was too late for them and life had distorted everything – and, of course, she had never dreamed that he would be forced out against his will. Neither of them had anticipated this grisly end.

When the staff cuts came, James was one of the first to be made redundant. Naturally he was plied with lame excuses: that huge reductions had had to be made and, while he had been a superb leader, while he had done his very best, while he had proved himself beyond measure in the Gulf, he had failed his staff exams; that, despite the fact that it had been mooted at the end of the Gulf War that he was going to be put up for the Military Cross because no lives had been lost in his squadron, there were others who were more proficient.

James was winded with the shock. He felt as if his life's blood was being drained from him. That the Army should desert him now, after seventeen years' service, was incomprehensible. The fear of the future was incapacitating. They tried to soften the blow by giving him a year's sabbatical but that almost made it worse. He had a whole year to contemplate the empty abyss that represented his future, and the rest of his life to wonder whether his love for Diana had in fact been worth it. After all, he had risked everything and been left with nothing.

He knew the real reason for his dismissal, of course. He was not fooled by these autocratic words, by the chuntering of the bureaucracy. He was well aware that it was his relationship with the Princess of Wales that, thanks to the adverse publicity that the papers were full of, had written his death warrant, that he was seen to be bringing the honourable name of the Life Guards into disrepute.

All he had ever wanted to do was to serve his country; ever since he had been a young boy he had dreamed of being a soldier. And now, as he saw it, because he had tried to do his duty, had tried to help his country by helping the wife of the future monarch to survive, he was being denied all that he had ever wanted. His men who he had thought would stand by him, loyal men who had willingly followed him into battle when he could have been leading them to their deaths, were turning their backs on him now. Without his army commission he was nothing, nobody.

He returned home to Devon thoroughly ashamed. He knew that his mother would not judge him, that her love was unconditional, but still he felt humiliated. It was unbearable that he had failed her. She was not emotionally open enough to tell him that she loved him, loved him so much he could never fail her, that all she had ever wanted was his happiness and that what hurt her, far more than his dismissal, was his present unhappiness; but she hoped that her mere unquestioning acceptance of him left him in no doubt. She never really mentioned what had happened, never allowed any disappointment to enter her voice, and this restraint was indication enough of her unswerving love for him.

His father too was stalwart – and James knew what high hopes he had had for him, how often he had told him that he was destined to command. That both his parents were so good to him made him feel weak inside. It made him feel like a small boy who had been so naughty that it had been quietly decided that there would be no punishment, that the consequences of his crime were punishment enough. He had wanted to be a success for them, had wanted to repay them for all they had always done for him and, more than anything, he had wanted them to be proud of him. Their cheery kindness in the face of his failure made the pain worse.

He tried to put on a brave face. No one discussed his future as they did not want to churn up further worry. As far as possible they went through the motions of the day as if nothing had happened. Their great British stoicism scarcely faltered.

Most of James's friends swiftly deserted him. As his love for Diana had been a secret, as no one had known the extent to which he had suffered, they misjudged him. They wrote him off as an unsatisfactory army officer and a weak fool, unaware that he had acted with unconditional kindness and patience. He may have been weak but he did not deserve this. Suddenly his presence at smart dinner parties was no longer required and the once steady stream of invitations dried up. He was exiled and alone.

The few friends who stuck by him tried their best to chivvy him along, telling him to pull himself together, not to give up, that something would turn up. Most of all they urged him to find a wife and to settle down, that he would feel more responsible and regain a sense of purpose if he had a family to care for. After all, he was a kind man who liked children, a generous godfather who surely wanted children of his own. He would be a natural father. If only he could end his bachelor days, life would take on a new meaning.

James thought about this and decided that perhaps they were right. Anything would be preferable to this fear and despair, and perhaps if he could learn to feel again things would improve. If he could just alert his emotions, he would feel better.

However, instead of allowing a kind, homely girl to soothe him and give him some stability, instead of falling for one of the many sweet horsy girls in his Devon circle, he rushed straight out and found almost a carbon copy of Diana. Just as Diana had turned to the available man most like Charles when she was hurting, James found the available woman most like Diana.

On some level he must have believed that he deserved to be punished for his affair with Diana. Deep down, because of his rigid background and military training, he felt that he had done wrong. He should have walked away, he told himself; he should not have got involved. Yet love had got the better of him; he had fallen in love and had discovered to his cost that it is the strongest emotion. It had overridden everything – his rationality and his fear.

So now, as if he were not being punished enough, he would punish himself further, would beat himself with the stick of his self-hatred. When he needed it least, when he should have kept his profile low, he sought out a woman who would bring him yet more adverse publicity. It was as if his antennae were on full alert for the potentially most damaging opportunity, and when he saw the red light, he simply accelerated.

He met Sally Faber, the wife of Conservative MP David Faber, out riding with the South Devon hunt. Just as he had with Diana, he struck up a friendship with Sally through the saddle. As they rode together they talked and, as they talked, Sally told James her story. Her need was familiar, her pain accessible. James had tasted that pain before; it may have burned him, but it had felt right and he was ready to taste it again. It was addictive – it was all he knew.

As Diana had, Sally explained that she was locked into a loveless marriage. She had been married to old Etonian David Faber for five years and now they barely communicated. She had met him when she was taking a secretarial course in Oxford and he was studying modern languages at the university. They had seemed an ideal couple: she was blonde and pretty, he was eligible and ambitious. Soon after the birth of their son, Henry, the glamour had faded. Sally found David cold and unyielding. She was lonely and she was playing a role; sustaining her veneer was exhausting her.

It was a language that James understood. They were words he had heard before. He knew what to do, knew how to cope. Automatically he became the supportive shoulder, the willing sounding board. The signals that had attracted him to Diana were there: the vulnerability, the pain, the sadness and the fear. That James could be of assistance made him feel useful again, made him feel manly.

Before he had time to think, he was back in the same old routine: the surreptitious telephone calls, the clandestine meetings, the snatched clinches and the quick caresses. There was the detailed planning, the waiting until the coast was clear and the unflagging vigilance.

It was as if, because James had only ever known a secret love, because he had never experienced true passion except silently behind a door kept ajar for the sound of the returning car, he did not know that love could be open and exposed. The idea was unfamiliar and scary; he did not know those rules. He did not know what it was like to walk into a room as one half of a bona fide couple, because he had entered so many rooms, for so many years, alone. He did not know what it was like to be able to share your joys, to scream out your feelings, because he had only ever kept his voice low and himself in check.

In fact, outside his army life, he had long ago forgotten that he had a voice. He had become so used to placating women, so used to giving in for fear that denying them anything might hurt them, that he could not remember what it was like to put himself first. He did not know how it would feel to act from a position of strength. At thirty-five he did not know what he wanted, let alone how to achieve it.

He had been so conditioned by Diana that he had gone headlong into the arms of another damaged woman who was hurt and could lash out. James may have told himself that after Diana he would have found a quiet, homely woman boring – that, in her own way, Sally, a television weather presenter, was also exotic and exciting – but perhaps in the solid, undemanding arms of a more selfless girl, in that form of boredom, he might have found a kind of peace.

This way he made sure that he could never relax. He would wait on tenterhooks, as he had done for years with Diana, until he was found out. He may have thought that he wanted commitment, that it was marriage he was after, but the mere fact that he chose a relationship with another married woman was evidence to the contrary. He had not changed; he was scared of commitment. He still felt safer sitting in the pews of life; he was not ready to stand at the top of the aisle.

Sally, like Diana, was relieved to have found this quiet, loving man. Unlike her husband, he made her feel special. Over the years she had begun to feel slightly unwelcome in the Faber family, as if she was not quite good enough, and it had diminished her. Now, in James's arms, she felt accepted, truly loved.

James could never meet the level of Sally's love. He was attracted to her and he worried for her because she was unhappy, but after Diana he had closed off. He genuinely wanted to help Sally and he longed for her to be happy, but he was deluding himself that they had a future together. It was too soon; he was in too much pain to give her what she needed, to let her near. He could not tell Sally about Diana, could not reveal that emotionally he was in despair; he could not tell anybody. He had lost faith in people, and in the process he had forgotten how to trust them.

Perhaps the only person who saw all of this, who thoroughly understood his state of mind, was his mother, and her insight frightened her. As she watched him igniting another time bomb, she prayed for his safety. Silently, she resented Sally and she wished that he was not so weak. She wished that he would stand up for himself and walk away. With Diana it had been different. Shirley Hewitt had truly loved Diana and she had seen that, in her way, Diana had loved James. She had seen the softness in Diana, the naïve optimism and the generosity of spirit.

Sally, as James was slowly discovering, was not the same. Although like Diana's her parents had divorced when she was a child, she did not come from the same type of sheltered, privileged background. Her eyes had been forced open earlier and her survival instinct was tougher. She had a hardness that Diana had never had. She may have been bitterly disappointed to discover that she had made a mistake in her marriage, but it had not touched her as Diana's had. She was more worldly when she married, more aware of what she was doing. The core of her had not been damaged because she had learned at an early age to protect herself, had decided long ago that she had to put herself first.

After a few months of seeing Sally, James knew that he was in too deep and that he could not cope. He was ensnared in another trap from which there was no clean way out. What his mother had feared was now plain to see. Hearts would be broken and lives disrupted.

He felt guilty that to appease Sally, in saying the words that she had wanted to hear, he had promised her more than he could ever honour. He was a fool to have led her to believe that he would marry her, and now he was afraid and sorry. For how could he possibly marry Sally when he was still in love with Diana? How could he marry anyone when Diana filled all his thoughts? When it was Diana whom he longed to hear whenever the telephone rang?

And how could he marry another woman when, still, he could deny Diana nothing; when, if Diana was feeling low and she asked him to tea at Kensington Palace, he still went running? It never crossed his mind to refuse her.

When the gossip columns tittered about his friendship with Sally, he told Diana the plain truth. He thought that he owed her that, that it was only fair. Her jealousy relieved and excited him. It gave him hope and boosted his confidence to know that she still cared. Now he knew that he could not stay with Sally and that he had to escape and try to find some fresh air.

He decided to go on a trip to Africa, and asked his old friend Francis Showering to accompany him. Together they bought an old Land Rover and drove the length of the continent. Sally was hurt when he told her that he needed space, that he needed time to think, but for the first time in his life James put himself first. He was too bruised to attend to her now.

He was slightly scared at the prospect of a couple of months of introspection under the vast open skies of Africa, but he thought that if only he could find himself, could learn to like and accept the man that he was, he might find the strength he needed. He had watched Diana take herself off and examine herself, had witnessed her dissecting her emotions, and he thought that if he could just do the same, he, like her, might stand more of a chance in life.

Ever since he had left school he had been burdened by responsibilities. This was the first time that he had felt free to attend to himself. Ever since his father had left home he had felt a tremendous sense of responsibility to women: to his mother, to his sisters, then to Diana and now to Sally. Leaving the Army had relieved him of his duties to his men and now he could travel unshackled, could leave the women, the regiment and the royal family behind. It was a relief to be just with Francis, who was possibly the only man who understood him. He felt so comfortable with him and enjoyed the camaraderie of setting up camp each night and organising their provisions. Of course, he ran the whole trip as if he was on a military exercise, but it did not feel like a duty because he got a great sense of satisfaction from his discipline. It did not tax him, but the familiarity of routine made him feel secure.

Francis could not have been a more sensitive companion. He

did not question him, did not force him to examine issues that he was not ready to face; he just let him be. If James wanted to talk, he would listen but he would not condemn. His mere presence was a measure of his friendship, of his support.

As he spent days behind the wheel, often in complete silence, James had time to consider his life. He felt strangely at home in Africa, this continent that was still quite wild. He was used to the smell of danger – he had walked on a precipice most of his adult life. He spent hours looking across the wide open landscape, studying the drama of the vistas ahead of him, trying to find out who he was. He had spent so long trying to be what everyone around him wanted him to be that he had no real sense of himself. He knew that he could give; he knew that he could make others happy but he did not know how to give to himself. He had no idea how to make *himself* happy.

After two months, Francis decided that he was missing his family too much, that he could not stay away from his wife and their young children any longer, and went home. James had not finished his quest, still did not have the true feel of himself, and, determined to keep trying, he carried on alone. After all, he thought, he could not possibly feel any more lonely than he already did, so what did it matter if he was alone? The threat of physical danger was nothing; nothing could ever hurt him as badly as he had been hurt before. If anything, physical hardship helped, because it took the edge off his emotional suffering.

He returned to England eventually in early December, having spent the whole autumn away. He was hardly any better off. He had not found himself because he had nothing to give himself. After the pain and humiliation that he had endured through loving Diana and trying to help her and then in being forced out of the Army, he had closed down so tightly that even he could not contact himself. He suspected that for the rest of his life he would be misunderstood, that people would point a jeering finger without knowing the truth.

On his return to England he soon walked into a storm of publicity over his relationship with Sally Faber. Completely without precedent, David Faber announced in the House of

Commons that he intended to divorce his wife and James was cited as the reason. It was an accusation that was later retracted but the public opprobrium would continue.

James had been to see Sally because he had to tell her that he could not give her what he knew she wanted and then, after the tears and the recriminations, came her husband's statement. James rushed back to London to be with her but his support was half-hearted. He was too afraid of his own future to know what to do.

While he was in Africa he had heard that the Prince and Princess of Wales had separated. As soon as he had been able, he had telephoned Diana to congratulate her. He was genuinely pleased for her as it seemed that her wish had been granted. Perhaps, finally, she would find the happiness she had craved, the peace she had worked so hard for.

Diana sounded flat and low on the telephone. When James said that he was delighted that she had got what she wanted, she replied that she did not think that it would ever be possible for her to have what she really wanted. She wondered if she would ever be truly happy. She felt that she was walking in the right direction, but she did not know if she would ever reach her goal.

In James's absence, Diana had surely realised that the love affair she had had with him was really the love affair that she had wanted to have with Charles; with great sadness, she had realised that she had made the same mistake and had reopened the same wounds. For in James she had thought that she had found strength, but in fact he, like Charles, was weak.

Was he out there, that prince whom she felt she deserved? She may have strayed but she had been punished. She had been so unhappy for such a long time. Was it so wrong that she had turned to James? Wasn't it brave that after Charles's rejection she had found the courage to trust again? Was it so terrible that she had sought some comfort and some happiness? Wasn't it clear that if her husband had loved her as she had loved him, she would never have walked away?

James put down the telephone and sat alone with his head in his hands. It was so very, very sad that they both seemed destined to walk parallel paths alone. For he suspected that he would walk alone for the rest of his life. The world would judge him harshly in its ignorance, when all he was was a kind, weak man who had done his very best.

Part of him still dreams of finding that friendly, loving woman with whom he might share his life, a warm friend who wants a house filled with flowers, children and dogs and a stable yard full of horses, a companion with whom he might find a form of peace. Yet he is afraid of that, afraid of hurting that woman who might come to him, but who could never have Diana's magic. Without his ever articulating it, without so much as a tepid look from him, she would instinctively know that he could never love her as he once loved and is still capable of loving. For he knows that once you have lived with tragedy and once you have known true happiness, nothing can take their place.